Turning Average Instruction into Great Instruction

School Leadership's Role in Student Achievement

John O'Connor

*Published in partnership with the American
Association of School Administrators*

ROWMAN & LITTLEFIELD EDUCATION
Lanham • New York • Toronto • Plymouth, UK

Published in the United States of America
by Rowman & Littlefield Education
A Division of Rowman & Littlefield Publishers, Inc.
A wholly owned subsidary of
The Rowman & Littlefield Publishing Group, Inc.
4501 Forbes Boulevard, Suite 200, Lanham, Maryland 20706
www.rowmaneducation.com

Estover Road
Plymouth PL6 7PY
United Kingdom

British Library Cataloguing in Publication Information Available

Library of Congress Cataloging-in-Publication Data

O'Connor, John, 1965-
  Turning average instruction into great instruction : school leadership's
role in student achievement / John O'Connor.
      p. cm.
  Includes bibliographical references.
  ISBN-13: 978-1-57886-948-0 (cloth : alk. paper)
  ISBN-13: 978-1-57886-949-7 (pbk. : alk. paper)
  ISBN-13: 978-1-57886-950-3 (electronic : alk. paper)
  ISBN-10: 1-57886-948-X (cloth : alk. paper)
  ISBN-10: 1-57886-949-8 (pbk. : alk. paper)
  ISBN-10: 1-57886-950-1 (electronic : alk. paper)
  [etc.]
  1. Effective teaching—United States. 2. Academic achievement—United
States. 3. Classroom management—United States. I. Title.
  LB1025.3.O28 2008
  371.102—dc22   2008040371

⊗™ The paper used in this publication meets the minimum requirements
of American National Standard for Information Sciences—Permanence of
Paper for Printed Library Materials, ANSI/NISO Z39.48-1992.
Manufactured in the United States of America.

This book is dedicated to Shawn, my wife,
and Luke and J. T., our sons.

Contents

List of Figures and Tables

Acknowledgments

I would like to thank Trenton Arnold, Karen Baron, Marlene Bryar, Owen Engelmann, Mary Jackson, John O'Dell, Betsy Primm, Bill Swan, Gloria Talley, Lynne Williams, and Frank Winstead for reviewing this book and making suggestions that were sorely needed.

Introduction: Focus

The ultimate goal in writing this book is to radically improve student achievement by focusing schools on the one critical factor that has the greatest impact on student achievement—classroom instruction. In fact, decades of research clearly show that what happens between teachers and students in our nation's classrooms has the greatest impact on how well those students learn.

In the educational arena, we have tried virtually every initiative and silver bullet available. We have adopted new programs, restructured schools, realigned organizational charts, and spent millions of dollars on quick fixes. At the end of the day, the element that must change in order to consistently increase student achievement is instruction, the interactions between teachers and students in classrooms.

In this book, specific components of effective instruction are described that should be seen in every classroom. I describe the components that turn average instruction into great instruction. However, the responsibility for school improvement is not placed solely on the shoulders of teachers. They certainly play a part—a big part. But the greater responsibility lies with school leaders: the central office staff, school principals, assistant principals, instructional coaches, school counselors, teacher leaders, and others who are responsible for establishing a clear vision for the school, setting priorities, and systematically taking steps toward that improvement.

Those of us who are leaders are responsible for creating and maintaining a school culture that provides teachers with the resources and the opportunity to acquire the skills to implement effective instruction. This book not only focuses on the elements of effective instruction, but also on the structures that must be built so that teachers, over time, consistently implement effective instruction.

Once we accept that improving student achievement relies largely on the instruction that occurs in classrooms, then we must realize that school improvement is completely reliant on our ability, as leaders, to improve the practices of our teachers. If we are successful at enhancing teachers' instructional practices, then we will be successful at improving student achievement. If we are unable to improve teacher practices, then we will be unsuccessful.

Therefore, this book not only includes the components of effective instruction but also describes how school leaders should develop the support, coaching, feedback, momentum, and direction needed for teachers to consistently improve their practices toward great instruction. I describe how school leaders can organize their faculty's efforts so that positive adult change ultimately leads to change in student performance.

Through the steps in this book, principals, assistant principals, and other administrators will be transformed from school administrators to instructional leaders. They will focus their school staff, set clear and consistent expectations for classroom instruction, organize personnel to provide layers of coaching and feedback, and systematically analyze adult practices and student performance. The role and impact of the school's leaders will be radically improved.

In addition to the specific "to do" list, this book includes a description of what schools need to stop doing. In fact, this may be the most challenging part of this book. Many activities are consuming the time and attention of our school leaders and teachers—often in the name of school improvement—that have virtually no impact on student achievement. School leaders must be challenged and encouraged to toss out those activities that are having little to no impact on student learning and to minimize those activities that are required but have little impact.

In other words, quit doing what does not work, but if you have to do some task that is required that will not have an impact, then get through with that activity as quickly as you can and get back to the tasks that will make a difference. In this book, school leaders are asked to be diligent about focusing on those activities that have a big impact on classroom instruction and, therefore, student achievement, and be courageous about removing or minimizing those activities that distract our teachers and leaders from focusing on effective instruction.

1

Overcoming Chaos

Thomas Logan was ecstatic when he found out he would be a father. Like most new dads, he realized that he needed some new skills. Even though he was pretty good around the house, his culinary talents were limited to making boxed macaroni and cheese, boiling hot dogs, and making PB & J sandwiches. He wanted the skills to whip up a meal that covered most food groups and exposed his child to a variety of tastes. Thomas registered for Cooking 101 and marked the first lesson on his calendar.

When he entered the cooking school's massive kitchen, he found chaos. The room itself was overwhelming. The expansive counter space was completely covered. Cooking utensils struggled to find space next to huge bags of raw materials. Pots and pans ranged in size from massive to quite small. There were cooking machines, some familiar and some less so. The blenders were easily recognized, but for a novice cook, many of the machines were quite foreign.

In addition to all of the cooking tools and utensils, there were ingredients everywhere. There were huge bags of flour and sugar. There were spices. There were vegetables and even meats. Thomas also noticed that the metal shelves were covered with three-ring binders titled *Cooking Improvement Plans*.

The scene was so overwhelming that Thomas didn't initially pay much attention to the people in the room. The dozen or so cooking students were furiously trying to cook their own respective dishes. Even though they were all participants in the same cooking class, they all seemed to be working on extremely different activities. In fact, they were all working furiously, but seemingly working in opposition to one another.

They were certainly giving it their all, but it didn't seem that they were very efficient at their task—probably because there were four master chefs all giving different orders. One of the chefs was directing the students to simmer sauces while the other chef ordered them to chop vegetables. The two other chefs were making other demands. The entire scene could only be described as chaos.

In actuality, this story never happened, but it does illustrate what is occurring in schools across the country. In the age of educational accountability, schools are expected to show high academic gains with their students. Virtually all schools are participating in school improvement activities. Schools are inundated with a variety of tools that are provided to help them with this process. There are computer programs that help schools analyze data. There are curriculum guides and pacing charts, how-to books and school reviews.

There are also plenty of "helpers" in our schools. Many of these professionals have the word "coach" in their title. There are instructional coaches, graduation coaches, change coaches, math coaches, and literacy coaches. There are also lead teachers. There are lead teachers for special education, lead math teachers, lead English teachers, and department chair persons.

There are also external supporters, many of whom are provided by State Departments of Education. In South Carolina (South Carolina Department of Education n.d.) and Georgia (Georgia Department of Audits 2007) for example, personnel hired by the State Department of Education provide on-site support and coaching in order to assist schools in increasing student achievement. In addition, schools have school administrators such as assistant principals for instruction who are dedicated to improving instruction in order to increase student achievement.

The expectations for school principals have also changed. At one point, they were expected to manage an orderly school. Now they are held responsible for meeting the accountability requirements based on increasingly higher expectations for student achievement.

If a school does not meet those requirements, then the school can be labeled as a "needs improvement" school. If the lack of success continues for multiple years, then a principal can lose his/her position and the school can be mandated to be restructured. There are also school improvement plans that sit in three-inch binders on administrators' shelves. Thousands of person-hours have gone into developing plans that could rival a Shakespearean play for complexity or a dictionary for length.

Like the cooks in the hypothetical kitchen, educators are working extremely hard—almost at a feverish pitch. Why then aren't all schools showing drastic improvement in student achievement? The answer is that many of the schools are approaching school improvement with an enormous amount of inefficiency. Effort is splintered endlessly as the various tools are utilized and the coaches, administrators, and external supporters move in different directions. Neither the documents nor the coaches are necessarily negative in and of themselves. In fact, many of the professionals are quite gifted at their task of supporting school personnel.

The problem occurs when the various activities and personnel are layered one upon the other seemingly in competition with each other. The efforts are not streamlined or even pointed in the same direction. In many cases, many of those activities are not focused on the most critical element for improving student achievement—systematically and effectively improving classroom instruction. New "programs" are implemented, complex administrative processes are put in place, and endless meetings occur, but the core issue of improving classroom instruction is missed. This approach will not enable teachers to impact student achievement any more than the master chefs in the scenario were able to lead the development of a great meal.

CHOOSING THE MEMBERS OF THE LEADERSHIP TEAM

Throughout this book, there are Questions for Reflection at the conclusion of each chapter. The questions are designed to help the reader analyze the activities of his/her school to determine if the school is effectively and efficiently implementing activities that will ultimately result in a radical improvement in student achievement. It is ideal to complete this book and the post-chapter questions with the leadership team from your school.

That team should include the principal, assistant principals, counselors, central office representatives, and teacher leaders from every department or grade in the school. It may also be helpful to include members of the community such as business partners and parent groups in this activity. The selection of the individual members of the leadership team will be very important as you work through this book. Their roles in this process will be very specific depending on their job title.

The principal should lead this effort because he/she has a unique role that only he/she can accomplish. The principal sets the tone of urgency and expectations for the entire school. The principal should provide clear direction and expectations for his/her leadership team and the rest of the staff. This role cannot be delegated. Many school initiatives have failed because they have been completely driven by someone other than the principal, like the assistant principal. Unfortunately, the assistant principal, no matter how talented, does not warrant the attention of the principal.

The message of urgency and priority must come from the principal. He/she must stand in front of the school faculty and stress the importance of the initiative and clearly articulate the expectations for the school. He/she must make it clear repeatedly that in his/her school an unwavering focus on improving and fine-tuning instruction is the first priority. The details of the initiative can be delegated to other personnel, but the principal must set the foundation and expectations. The school staff will only participate in school improvement efforts, including the completion of this book, to the extent that the principal leads the effort and emphasizes its importance.

All of the assistant principals in your school (regardless of their title) should participate in this process. In many larger schools, there are assistant principals for instruction, assistant principals for attendance, assistant principals for discipline, and so forth. Unfortunately, a barrier has been created with those titles. Many school personnel assume that improving instruction is the sole responsibility of the administrator who has the term "instruction" in their title.

Many teachers—and the assistant principals themselves—believe that none of the other assistant principals bear any responsibility for improving instructional practices or improving student achievement. All assistant principals are responsible for improving instruction throughout the school. All administrators need to be in the game. They must work together to provide consistent support and coaching to teachers as they try new instructional techniques and re-flect on those strategies. Each administrator, including every assistant principal, must be transformed from school administrator to instructional leader.

The leadership team should also include all support personnel such as counselors, school psychologists, and the like. Nobody should be exempt from improving instructional activities in the school. If any certified personnel suggest that their job does not impact classroom instruction, then it is worthwhile to analyze the impact they are having at the school. These individuals will be critical as coaching and momentum is established. Their expertise can also be quite valuable during the processes outlined throughout this book.

There must also be some careful consideration when choosing the teachers who will participate in this and other school improvement processes. In addition to department chairs, representatives from each area (e.g., special education and English language learners), and other official teacher leaders, the team should include teachers who have great influence. Some superteachers have a positive impact on any initiative in the school. They volunteer for many activities and find a way to "get the job done" regardless of the challenges that arise. They should definitely be included on the leadership team.

Other teachers who have influence, perhaps even negative influence, should also be included on the leadership team. There are some teachers in many schools who have taught at the school for years, have long-standing institutional knowledge, and have strong influences on other teachers. They may even express resistance to most new ideas. Those teachers should be on the leadership team that works through this book even though their influence might be less than positive. As long as their influence is not poisonous, it is critical to gain their acceptance on the front end of this initiative rather than trying to convince them of its value at a later date.

The leadership team that works together to complete this book should also include internal and external helpers. The instructional coaches, whether they are full-time school employees or based at the central office, should participate in this process. The instructional coaches (regardless of the title in your school) often receive direction from professionals outside of your school and bring effective ideas back to your school. Unfortunately, it is easy for their activities, no matter how sound, to lack alignment with your initiatives.

If they participate in your school's process of building effective instructional practices, then they can bring their new ideas to the leadership group and work in alignment with your efforts. Their activities will be implemented through the lens and overall plan of your efforts, rather than competing with your initiatives.

Your leadership team should include at least one professional from the central office. Like the instructional coaches, their ownership of the ultimate plan to improve instruction will strengthen your efforts. In many school districts, central office personnel are aware of available resources that can contribute to your teams' efforts to improve instruction. They may be aware of funding sources, individuals with expertise, and initiatives that would fold effectively in your overall plan. With their knowledge base and connections, central office personnel can contribute to the growth of your leadership team and the ultimate implementation of any school improvement initiative.

All of the members of the expanded leadership team should work collaboratively to answer the questions at the end of each chapter in this book.

QUESTIONS FOR REFLECTION

Chapter 1: Overcoming Chaos

1. List the personnel who will read this book and collaborate to develop answers to the questions at the end of each chapter. Include all administrators, support personnel, department chairs, other teacher leaders, and teachers who represent various programs in the school (e.g., special education). Include all teachers who have significant influence on their colleagues. In addition, include internal and external instructional coaches who work in your school and central office personnel whose connections and knowledge can contribute to your efforts.
2. Describe the school improvement efforts that are being undertaken in your school. Include a description of the initiatives that are in place and how the various leadership personnel are involved. Are these efforts aligned and resulting in consistent improvements in student achievement or are the tireless efforts resulting in a lack of corresponding increases in student achievement? Support your answers with an explanation.

3. In your school, are the school improvement efforts bordering on a sense of chaos or is there a strong sense of order and aligned purpose toward improving classroom instruction? Whether your answer involves chaos or order, describe the elements that are contributing to that result.

2

GREAT Instruction

Educators across the country are scratching their heads over how to increase the achievement of all students in their buildings. Traditionally, some student subgroups have done well while other subgroups have underperformed. Educators are required to focus on every group of students in their schools. According to the No Child Left Behind legislation (2002), a growing percentage of students in each school and each school district must meet or exceed specific academic expectations in the curriculum. In most states, students demonstrate this achievement by passing statewide assessments in various subject areas.

The No Child Left Behind legislation does not focus solely on raising the average score across the school or the overall percentage of students who meet or exceed the passing score. Instead, it focuses on every subgroup of students. The scores from each subgroup, individual ethnic groups for example, are reported and that group must have an increasing percentage of students who meet or exceed expectations.

If even one subgroup does not meet expectations over time, then the entire school can be labeled as a "Needs Improvement" school. The subgroups include all ethnic groups, students with disabilities, students from economically disadvantaged families, and students with Limited English Proficiency (also known as English language learners). Therefore, the accountability status of each school hinges on the performance of each student subgroup.

How can a school ensure that each of those subgroups, some of which have been traditionally underserved by public education, meet, or better yet exceed, expectations? The answer to this question is fairly obvious. All students need one thing to perform at high levels—great instruction. Fair instruction or even good instruction is not sufficient to improve the academic achievement of every student.

In actuality, some children enter school and can perform sufficiently with mediocre instruction. A small percentage of children actually learn to read spontaneously. When they are about three years old, they look at a book and realize that they have broken the code. All of those lines that used to look like squiggles now mean something. Those lines are letters. Those letters spell out words and those words tell a story.

Lynn Holland (personal communication, November 9, 2005) remembers that magical moment when she was three years old and it happened to her. She opened a book and all of a sudden, she could read. She remembers running down the hallway and telling her mother that she could read the book. She even remembers that it was a Winnie the Pooh book. How amazing!

To be honest, children who come to school with these skills can probably do well with passable instruction, especially in their primary school years. Other children, especially those who come from traditionally underserved groups such as students with disabilities, students from economically disadvantaged circumstances, and other students who struggle need great instruction. In fact, nothing else will make a significant impact on the academic achievement of all students.

What are the components of "great" instruction? If each of the teachers in your school were asked what constitutes great instruction, how many answers would you get? In many schools, you would get as many answers as you have teachers. Why do public schools allow every teacher to determine the components of great instruction? That seems like an inefficient way to move in the same direction. Does that lack of a clear vision seem similar to the scenario in the industrial kitchen? Are the teachers in your school working extremely hard, but lacking efficiency because they are implementing instructional strategies that they think are appropriate but are less than effective?

A combination of research and school-based experiences tells us that there are specific components that make up great instruction. GREAT instruction should be:

- Guided by the curriculum
- Rigorous with research-based strategies
- Engaging and exciting
- Assessed continuously to guide instruction, and
- Tailored through flexible groups.

GUIDED BY THE CURRICULUM

In most states, there is a curriculum that has been defined by the State Department of Education. That curriculum has specific performance standards that clearly outline the expectations for children in different subjects and in different grades. Instruction should be aligned to the performance standards in that curriculum. School districts usually have some flexibility in the choice of materials and textbooks adopted to address that curriculum.

Unfortunately, in many classrooms teachers assume that their curriculum is defined by the textbook series. They complete chapter after chapter in the text and therefore believe they are appropriately addressing the curriculum. In fact, those materials are merely tools that can be used to assist students in mastering the components or standards of the curriculum.

Teachers need to have a deep knowledge of the competencies that students are expected to master by the end of the course or school year. They need to have a clear understanding of what the finish line looks like. They need to know how children will demonstrate those skills and competencies. They need to know when that demonstration is sufficiently complex to meet the expected standard.

Just as important, they need to have a clear understanding of when that demonstration of skillfulness does not meet the expectancy of the standard. What is the very fine line between being competent in each standard and being just below the bar? On the other end of the performance continuum, how can a student show that he/she exceeds the curricular standards? How can he/she rise above the expectations and demonstrate even deeper understanding and skillfulness? What is the end point for those students who can meet that greater challenge?

A thorough understanding of the curriculum prepares teachers for their day-to-day work with their students. If instruction is developed and delivered for the purpose of achieving the curricular standards, then teachers will be able to identify the students who are not on track to meet those standards a few weeks into instruction.

Through that deep knowledge and clear alignment with the curriculum, teachers will be able to alter instruction depending on their students' progress. They will be able to ramp up instruction when it is necessary, reteach material at other times, and expect more complexity when students need more challenges. With a clear understanding and vision of the curricular standards, teachers can build effective instructional activities that lead to successfully reaching academic expectations.

RIGOROUS WITH RESEARCH-BASED STRATEGIES

Rigor

GREAT instruction should also be rigorous. Many people assume that students who struggle in school need less rigorous instruction. They assume that those students who have disabilities, those from economically challenging circumstances, or other students who struggle need less rigorous instruction or less challenging expectations than their more successful peers. That, in fact, is quite wrong.

Students who are lagging behind their peers or who struggle need more rigorous instruction. Schools need to provide instruction that will allow them to catch up to their peers. They will have to learn at a faster rate than their classmates who are on grade level. The students not only need to master the same curricular standards as their peers, but they must also fill in those academic holes that they have developed over time.

They may need to be explicitly taught learning strategies to attack math word problems when other students may attain those metacognitive skills fairly naturally. They may need to be taught how to decode multisyllabic words when other students already have those skills. They may need to learn organizational skills when other students already know how to break down tasks to increase learning. Struggling students or students who are lagging behind their peers need to learn more than other students in the same amount of time. Therefore, their instruction needs to be more rigorous, not less so.

All students should become sophisticated problem solvers—all students at all grade levels. We, as educational leaders and teachers, can only reach that goal with rigorous instruction and high expectations. First grade instruction as well as instruction for seniors in high schools should include opportunities for students to attempt solutions to various challenges and to weigh those solutions against the challenge. Of course, expectations should be developmentally appropriate for students at various ages while promoting the use of higher order thinking skills rather than surface level information.

One barrier to rigorous instruction is suppressed expectations. Many schools aim much too low by focusing almost exclusively on meeting the minimum required score on the statewide assessments. You will hear entire faculties talk about the magical "passing" score on the state test. Unfortunately, that passing score is what it takes for a student to show that he/she barely meets expectations for his/her grade. In many states, that bar is surprisingly low.

Focusing on the minimum proficiency score can actually decrease student achievement. Instead of solely striving to assist struggling students to meet that minimum mark, schools should strive toward getting more students to significantly exceed that score. If more students exceed expectations, then even those students who struggle will surpass the minimum score.

In addition to "pushing" students from the tail end of the spectrum to just pass the test, school personnel should also "pull" the top students into even higher ranges so that all students shift to a higher level of performance. All students show growth and therefore all scores shift upward. Students who are doing well continue to show growth and students who are struggling meet or exceed the minimum requirements. Take a look at the array of scores from a hypothetical school that focuses solely on assisting students to make the minimum passing score of 800 on their statewide assessment. All teachers instruct all students in the hope that they will score at least 800 points on the annual assessment.

As a result of the teachers focusing on the minimum passing score, average students scored 800 points on the assessment and gifted students surpassed that score. Unfortunately, students who struggle scored below 800 points. This group of students will have a

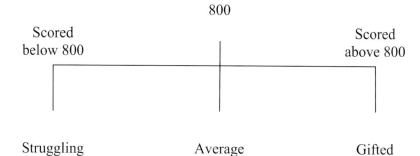

Figure 2.1.   Array of scores if teachers teach toward the minimum passing score

significant impact on whether the school is able to meet the bench-marks in the accountability standards.

As mentioned previously, if enough struggling students come from the same student group (e.g., students with disabilities, English language learners, economically disadvantaged students, or students from the same ethnic group), then the school can ultimately be labeled as a "Needs Improvement" school. Now look at the same hypothetical school if teachers increase their rigor and "teach toward" the complexity of a score of 840 points.

When teachers increased the rigor in their classroom instruction and aimed for a score of 840 for all students, then the average students reached 840, the gifted students exceeded that score, and the struggling students met the state-defined minimum score of 800

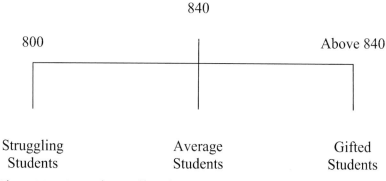

Figure 2.2.   Array of scores if teachers provide rigorous instruction

points. Essentially, all scores were moved to the right. These teachers pulled from the top as well as pushed from the bottom. Previously, they had only pushed students in order to get them over the 800 point threshold.

How can it be ensured that rigorous instruction and high expectations are occurring in classrooms? Rigorous instruction must start with the teachers' knowledge of the content area. According to the U.S. Department of Education (2006), research indicates that there is a connection between teachers' knowledge of their content area and their students' levels of achievement. This is the rationale behind the requirement in the No Child Left Behind legislation that teachers are "highly qualified" in every academic subject they teach.

Mathematics teachers, for example, must understand the complexities of their subject matter. They must be able to connect the various mathematical concepts at a deep level. It is not sufficient for mathematics teachers to merely understand how to compute figures. They must have a deep understanding of mathematical concepts, problem solving, and computational skills. They must possess this knowledge for their grade level and also for subsequent grade levels. That way they can equip their students with the necessary skills for long-term success in mathematics. A science teacher must not be one chapter ahead of his/her students. The teacher must understand how science impacts all facets of life and should connect those everyday experiences with underlying scientific principles.

Teachers should also be cautioned about the potential misinterpretation of rigor in classrooms. Some teachers assume that providing rigorous instruction is merely the practice of expecting higher performance from students. They assume that having a harder class is equivalent to providing rigorous instruction. Some teachers, in fact, particularly in high schools, might brag that relatively few students make high grades: "The average grade on my science class was a 72."

Rigor does not reduce the obligation of the teacher to provide systematic and clear instruction. Merely offering harder work is not sufficient. Many students need explicit instruction. At the primary years, most students need explicit and systematic instruction in decoding in the area of reading. Throughout school, students must also be explicitly taught the problem-solving steps involved in approaching a mathematics word problem. Increased rigor must be accompanied with increased explicit instruction and support as students gain the skills to meet higher expectations.

The high school teacher who brags about the low performance rate of his/her students should reflect on why more students did not succeed. He/she should build explicit and systematic instruction and support for his/her students so they are able to meet rigorous expectations.

Research-based Instructional Strategies

GREAT instruction also includes the use of research-based instructional strategies. For far too long, educators have jumped on the latest instructional trend or gimmick. The educational community can be easily swayed by thin research, shiny brochures, quick headlines, or slick salespeople. When educators try to implement research-based instruction, they often rely exclusively on vendors' marketing information. Unfortunately, many vendor catalogs announce that their products are now "research based" whether or not there is any truth to that statement.

Since the term is bandied about so freely, it makes sense to ask, "What exactly does 'research based' mean?" It depends on who you ask. Many educators would say that anything that is published could be described as "research based." There are many journals and books (this being one) that are published but certainly do not meet the criteria of having been the product of "scientifically based research." These publications (hopefully including this one) can be very useful in helping schools implement effective practices, but they do not warrant the descriptor of "scientifically based research."

The No Child Left Behind legislation (2002) defined the components of "scientifically based research." Among other criteria, the legislation stated that "scientifically based research" includes:

- Randomized assignment of participants to various conditions
- Replicable studies
- Reliable and valid data across evaluators and observers, across multiple measurements, and across studies
- Rigorous data analysis that can effectively be used to draw a conclusion
- Systematic, empirical methods
- Objective and systematic procedures that can lead to valid and reliable conclusions.

In essence, the definition of "scientifically based research" provided in the No Child Left Behind legislation describes the type of research that is often seen when a new medicine is being tested. To oversimplify, subjects are randomly assigned to multiple groups. The randomization of the participants, when completed sufficiently, minimizes the impact of the differences, or variables, between the various subjects. The subjects are then provided different interventions and their results are compared.

By using the medical approach, researchers can, to a point, state that the intervention had an impact on the changes in the subjects. The medicine, therefore, can be linked to improved health or a reduction of the symptoms of a particular medical condition. If multiple studies are conducted by various researchers and a particular intervention is connected to groups with better outcomes, then it can be stated that the intervention has scientifically based research to support it.

In the educational arena, this type of research can be used to determine whether an instructional strategy has a link to increased learning. A particular reading strategy might be compared to other strategies to determine if it increases reading comprehension, for example. Did multiple research studies reveal that students who received the particular instructional strategy demonstrate more growth in reading comprehension than the comparison groups? If so, then the instructional strategy can be described as being supported with scientifically based research. This is a very high bar or as some would say the "gold standard" of research.

What are some of the scientifically based instructional strategies that should be seen in elementary schools where one of the primary goals is to teach students to become effective readers? According to the National Reading Panel, in 1997, the U.S. Congress became concerned about the lack of a consensus on effective reading instruction and asked the National Institutes of Health to establish a panel to review the effectiveness of various approaches to teach reading (About the National Reading Panel 2001).

After conducting a significant, although not exhaustive, review of the research in reading that met the standards of scientifically based research, the Panel determined that there are five core components beneficial in teaching reading. Those five dimensions of reading include instruction in phonemic awareness (the ability to recognize and manipulate the sounds in words), phonics, comprehension, fluency (the ability to read smoothly and quickly), and vocabulary. The panel recommended specific instructional strategies for each of these areas. Teachers should analyze students' skills in the five components and provide explicit instruction with research-based strategies to strengthen students' areas of weaknesses (National Institute of Child Health and Human Development 2000).

The amount of scientifically based research is very limited, unfortunately, in many academic content areas. Out of necessity, schools have to rely on instructional strategies that have undergone less strenuous research. The main recommendation here is to have someone on your staff or someone in your school district who is knowledgeable about research-based strategies and can evaluate the claims made by vendors, researchers, or other schools.

These professionals must be given the opportunity to review the research and share their findings in clear, concise, and understandable ways. They may access information provided by independent entities that review educational research. For example, the What Works Clearinghouse (n.d.) provides objective reviews of research on specific educational and instructional interventions. The clearinghouse was established by the U.S. Department of Education's Institute of Education Sciences to provide information to educators with reliable information on educational research.

The professionals in your district who review the research should provide concise summaries of the recommendations. Those summaries should include specific descriptions of how the instructional strategies should be implemented in accordance with the research. Over time, the school district can adopt specific strategies, based on its own evaluation of the existing research, rather than relying on the claims of vendors or other professionals who have a financial, philosophical, or, at the very least, an emotional interest in a specific instructional strategy. In many cases, you will choose to support instructional strategies that do not meet the criteria of scientifically based research, but that does not mean that you should automatically accept anything that is in print.

Educators should be critical consumers in determining if recommendations have objective research to support them. Educators should also enlarge their information networks by asking schools that have implemented interventions and programs about the positive and negative aspects of the particular practices. A little bit of information about the actual implementation and success of initiatives can be quite informative.

When discussing instructional interventions with other schools, attempt to determine if reported improvements in student achievement were caused by specific instructional interventions. Many schools unwittingly alter other variables that may have had the positive impact.

Several years ago, one school reported that altering the classrooms (dimming the lights, playing soft music, etc.) for fourth grade students had an admirable impact on students' reading and math abilities. While describing the interventions, school administrators stated that they had "put our best teachers in the fourth grade to see if the altered classrooms would have an impact." In this scenario, improvements in student achievement were probably the result of the pooling of the talented teachers for the fourth grade rather than the changes made to the classroom setting.

What about the instructional strategies used in middle and high schools? In too many middle and high schools, two instructional strategies are overused: teacher lecture and student independent work. Many teachers alternate between lecturing students with information and then passing out assignments. There is certainly a place for both of these instructional strategies, but in many middle and high school classrooms they dominate the instruction.

In many math classes, for example, the teacher provides examples of math problems on a projector and then gives students assignments to complete independently. In and of itself, this can lead to low levels of learning. Students do need to have specific processes explicitly taught to them. Then they need the opportunity to try those processes out in a variety of contexts. Instead of only completing pages of math problems in geometry classes in high schools, for example, students need the opportunity to construct various structures quickly and determine how the various shapes and sizes intersect to change the structure's area.

Many researchers have recommended specific instructional strategies. Marzano, Pickering, and Pollack (2001), for example, report on their meta-analysis of instructional strategies and recommend nine classroom practices that have a positive impact on student learning. Those strategies are (1) identifying similarities and differences, (2) summarizing and note taking, (3) reinforcing effort and providing recognition, (4) homework and practice, (5) nonlinguistic representations, (6) cooperative learning, (7) setting objectives and providing feedback, (8) generating hypotheses, and (9) questions, cues, and advance organizers.

Fidelity

Choosing instructional strategies that are grounded in research meets only half of the challenge of effectively teaching. An equally important issue is whether teachers implement those instructional strategies with fidelity. All too often teachers are provided relatively limited opportunities to learn about new strategies through one-day workshops or professional conferences. They then try out those strategies and unknowingly implement them inaccurately.

They may not provide the instruction in the way that the strategies have been designed and studied. They may not provide sufficient intensity of instruction. They may not be implementing the instructional strategies with sufficient frequency, or providing appropriate feedback to students. Teachers must use research-based instructional strategies and implement those strategies with fidelity.

What can a school do to ensure that the research-based strategies they adopt are implemented with fidelity? A school or perhaps the school district must ensure that they have shared information about how specific strategies should be implemented. This information should be extremely concrete and specific. Teachers should be allowed to layer their own personality and style on the instructional strategy only as long as their implementation is within the parameters of how the instructional strategy has been studied and shown to be effective.

Implementation with fidelity is also impacted by the degree to which ongoing coaching and monitoring is provided. Teachers must be given opportunities to attempt their strategies, receive feedback on the implementation, brainstorm improvements, and refine the strategy implementation over time. These activities must be framed within a context of accountability and monitoring. In addition to providing coaching and support, school leaders must ensure that teachers' strategy implementation is steadily moving toward fidelity.

ENGAGING AND EXCITING

There is another component of GREAT instruction that is critically important, but is more difficult to quantify. Students need "magic."

They need to be pulled in and engaged in instruction. When you walk in some classrooms, this magic is apparent. You will see it from that magnificent second grade teacher who waits until his/her students are out of the room to place green construction-paper footprints all over the room.

When the students line up outside of the room to enter, the teacher looks astonished and says, "You won't believe what happened. A leprechaun visited our room when we were out. His footprints are everywhere (personal communication, L. Eggers November 15, 1993). And it looks like he left a story on everyone's desk. I'm not sure we should read the story. What do you think?" Of course the children will say almost in unison, "Yes. Let's read the story." The children will be pulled into the instruction. Their eyes will be shining and they will be completely enthralled in their activity.

You can also see this magic in middle and high school classrooms. A creative geometry teacher will not rely on worksheets to practice determining the area of various shapes. Instead, he/she will give the students the following assignment to solve in cooperative groups:

> Build a dog house for a full grown Sheltie. The height must exceed the width. The doghouse can include a cube, but can not exclusively be a cube. The area of the dog house must be as close to 1,142 cubic units as possible.

The teacher will then provide the students with a toy like Super Fort™, which is made by Cranium™. They are essentially noodles, typically used as floats in swimming pools, except they have magnets on each end. The students can quickly build a structure using these toys. Most important, they can easily tinker with the structure until they develop a final product. They will alternate between their mathematical equations and the structure and make adjustments until they have arrived at a reasonable answer for the problem.

The teacher will watch groups become completely engaged in their work and collaborate as teams work toward their final goal. Some students will immediately start building while other students will approach the challenge by solving mathematical problems on paper. The skillful teacher will quietly fade into the background to observe the students as they discuss and brainstorm their solutions.

The teacher will facilitate effective problem solving when needed, but will allow the students an opportunity to attempt and reattempt various options. The bell can ring and students will not want to abandon their work. This is "magic" and is a combination of teacher competence combined with enthusiastic, energetic, and engaging delivery of instruction. It is a combination of substance and style.

ASSESSED CONTINUOUSLY TO GUIDE INSTRUCTION

Instruction should also be continuously assessed through the use of progress monitoring of student learning. According to O'Connor and Williams (2006), for decades elementary schools have taught spelling in the same manner. On Monday, students receive a new list of spelling words. During the week, they complete a variety of activities including writing sentences with the words, defining the words, and perhaps playing spelling games. On Friday, the students take a spelling test.

What happens on the following Monday? All students receive a new set of words. In many cases, the results of Friday's spelling test have not been used to impact Monday's spelling words. All students receive the same list. Some students were competent in spelling all of the words before they were even assigned. They received a perfect score on their spelling test. Some students struggled and performed poorly on the spelling test, missing most of the words. Nonetheless, on the following Monday they all receive the same set of new words. The spelling test essentially serves one purpose—to provide a score for the teacher's grade book (O'Connor and Williams 2006).

The same phenomenon is also seen in high schools. Teachers provide instruction for two or three weeks, which is followed by a test or some type of project. The next day the teacher embarks on the next unit. The teacher does not use the results of the assessment to guide continued instruction. In fact, it often takes the teacher several days or even several weeks to grade the students' tests or projects. Again, the main purpose of the assessment is seemingly to determine a numerical grade for the teacher's grade book.

Teachers should implement progress monitoring measures to assess the progress of their students in comparison to the curriculum standards. According to L. Fuchs and D. Fuchs (n.d.), one type of progress monitoring is Curriculum Based Measurement (CBM), in which assessments are implemented that compare students' progress over time to the annual expectations of the curriculum. In elementary mathematics, for example, students take an assessment regularly that includes representative problems from the entire year's curriculum on mathematics. This type of CBM includes samples of each of the problem types that the student will see during the year. The specific problems will change, but their complexity throughout the year will remain consistent. Students are asked to answer all of the mathematical problems and their scores are compared over time.

With this approach, school personnel can graph and analyze students' progress compared to the expectations at the end of the year. The progress, or slope, of the number of correct digits in the students' responses is compared to ensure that the student is on course to meet expectations by the end of the school year. If the student's trend line is sufficiently steep (the percentage of correct digits on the problems) as the year progresses, there is visible evidence that the student is on course for year-end expectations. As the school year progresses, students will become more proficient in all types of problems and the graphed slope will gradually move upward. Fuchs and Fuchs (n.d.) state that in reading, spelling, and mathematics, there are over 200 empirical studies documenting the positive impact of progress monitoring.

Curriculum Based Measurement is also an effective process for secondary aged students. According to the National Center on Student Progress Monitoring (n.d.), the trend line for students' learning in reading can be charted by having students regularly complete a timed, three-minute maze passage. Their data graphs will demonstrate if their reading skills are progressing sufficiently (their graphed slope is sufficiently steep) to meet end-of-the-year curricular expectations. Similarly, progress monitoring for written expression can be effectively evaluated with a weekly, timed, five-minute writing sample in response to a prompt. For learning in content areas, progress monitoring can be accomplished by comparing students' responses on timed measures that have the students match vocabulary with their definitions.

Admittedly, the research that is available on Curriculum Based Measures is more substantial for students in early elementary school than for older students. In some instances, therefore, schools are developing common assessments that are devised and used by all of the teachers who teach the same grade/subject throughout the school (or course in high school). These common assessments are developed at the school or district level, rather than by individual teachers, to ensure that the assessments are aligned and adequately reflect the complexity of the curriculum.

Whichever approach is used, progress-monitoring measures should be reliable predictors of how students will perform on annual assessments. If students are not on course to meet those expectations, then teachers can analyze the assessment data and use it to adjust instruction to better meet the students' learning needs.

As teachers analyze their progress-monitoring data for individual students and across their class, they should ask, "Are there specific students who are struggling in my class? What needs to be retaught and how should I reteach that information? Are there specific students who are exceeding expectations? Are there trends across the class, either positive or negative? If so, what information does that provide about the instruction provided on those particular components and how does instruction need to be impacted as our class moves forward?"

TAILORED THROUGH FLEXIBLE GROUPS

Assessment to guide instruction, the "A" in GREAT instruction leads to the next component that should be seen in every classroom—differentiating or tailoring instruction through flexible grouping. This element is most often seen in the classrooms of powerful kindergarten and first grade teachers. When you observe an outstanding primary teacher, you will see students broken into various groups. The teacher utilizes a kidney-shaped table in the back of the room to provide instruction to one group of students while two other groups of students conduct meaningful activities.

If you ask that strong teacher why the students are grouped as they are, he or she will say something like, "This group needs assistance with decoding consonant-vowel-consonant words while that group needs assistance with their sight words." The teacher will then follow up with, "If you come back in a few weeks, you will see a different grouping pattern. I will shuffle the students as I continue to analyze their needs."

Unfortunately, as students get older, fewer teachers use flexible grouping in order to differentiate instruction. As mentioned earlier, middle and high school instruction is often limited to the teacher lecturing from the front of the room and then giving the students assignments they often complete independently. All teachers should have a keen understanding of students' ongoing levels of learning, based on progress monitoring, which in turn provides a basis for providing instruction in flexible groups.

Instruction in virtually every class, kindergarten through high schools, should involve large group instruction mixed with small group instruction that targets specific needs for the students in the groups. An observer should routinely see students placed in a variety of small groups and should be able to ask the teacher the rationale for the groupings. The expected response should be something like, "Those three students are having difficulty summarizing information from a technical text. Two students with them are very strong in that skill and needed additional challenges. Those two students are providing tutorial services to those three students a few minutes every day until they acquire those skills."

Using flexible groups is admittedly only one way to provide differentiation for students with various needs. A variety of instructional components can be differentiated. The way information is presented can be varied. The student activity can be customized and the type of work that students complete to demonstrate their proficiency can be altered depending on the needs of the students.

Remember that the ultimate purpose of this book is to enable school leadership teams to enhance the practices of their teaching staff so there are substantial improvements in student achievement. It would be difficult to observe a classroom and determine if teachers are using those other methods of differentiation in appropriate response to the results of ongoing assessments if flexible groups are not being implemented.

Utilizing flexible groups and facilitating discussion with the teachers about his/her rationale for those groups creates a context in which improvements in differentiation can become concrete. Therefore, utilizing flexible groups is recommended as the priority method for differentiating instruction. It will set the context in which teachers can differentiate instruction in systematic and purposeful ways.

In summary, all students need GREAT instruction. Gifted and talented students as well as students from groups that have been historically underserved in public education need GREAT instruction.

They will not meet their potential with mediocre instruction. That GREAT instruction must be:

Guided by the curriculum
Rigorous with **r**esearch-based strategies
Engaging and **e**xciting
Assessed continuously to guide instruction
Tailored through flexible groups

QUESTIONS FOR REFLECTION

Chapter 2: GREAT Instruction

1. In your school, if you asked every teacher what constitutes great instruction, how many answers would you get? If you arrive at a large number, why do you think that is?

2. Analyze the instructional practices across your school. Next to each of the elements for GREAT instruction estimate the percentage of classrooms in your school in which you see the component delivered with sufficient expertise. Explain your answers.

   Guided by the curriculum
   Rigorous with **r**esearch-based strategies
   Engaging and **e**xciting
   Assessed continuously to guide instruction
   Tailored through flexible groups

3

Changing Adult Practices

The premise of this book is that radically improving student achievement hinges on the GREAT instruction that teachers provide to their students. If every teacher in a school provides GREAT instruction, then students will achieve at higher levels. The success of our efforts to radically improve student achievement relies on one thing—our ability as leaders to effectively help teachers change their practices. As educational leaders, if we are effective at improving teachers' ability to provide GREAT instruction, then we will see increased academic performance by our students.

If we are unable to improve teachers' practices, then we will see the same results that we saw previously. The same students who have traditionally been successful will continue to be successful. The same groups of students who have been underserved by public education will continue to underperform. The logic is really very simple—if we want to see significant improvements in achievement, then we have to focus our efforts on improving and ensuring teachers' practices. Even though the logic is simple, improving teacher practices is anything but easy.

The next question is obvious. What does it take to change teachers' practices? The answer can be found at your nearest martial arts studio. Let's say that a woman named Elisha is interested in taking martial arts classes. In fact, she has decided to dedicate herself to earning a black belt. She was athletic in high school but became less active as she got older. She not only decides that she wants to earn a black belt, but she also sets a timeline for herself. She sets an ambitious goal of earning that black belt in two years. What does she need to do to improve her "practices" or skillfulness so that she steadily grows as a martial artist, ultimately earning a black belt?

The obvious answer is that Elisha needs practice—lots of it. But she needs other elements also. She needs to find a martial arts studio whose coaches have a history of effectively training adults to become black belts. By finding a studio with that history, she will be sure she participates in an "evidenced-based" curriculum, proven effective in assisting the participants in reaching their goals.

It will not serve her purpose to sign up with a martial arts studio that primarily focuses on five- and six-year-old potential martial artists who quickly lose interest in the sport. She needs to be trained by professionals who have established a pattern of assisting athletes in acquiring their black belts.

By enrolling in an established, effective martial arts studio, she can be sure her coach has a clear vision of the end goal. The coach will know specifically what skills Elisha needs to develop. The coach clearly understands the specific competencies for earning a black belt. She has to become adept at performing specific kicks and punches. She needs to complete predetermined sequences of martial arts movements that combine to make a whole. She needs competence in sparring and blocking. Her coach must have a clear and very specific understanding of what Elisha will need to learn and be able to do over the next two years. As Elisha moves through this process, her understanding of those black belt competencies will also become clear and concrete.

In collaboration with her coach, Elisha also needs to determine her starting point. They need to determine her strengths and weaknesses near the onset of her quest. They will determine where she stands on elements like flexibility, strength, and coordination. Based on this analysis, her instructor will undoubtedly try to capitalize on her strengths while improving her areas of weaknesses. If she is extremely flexible but has poor body strength, she will certainly continue to stretch before every practice and will have a good range of motion in her kicks, but she will spend extra time and energy on improving her body strength. This initial assessment will help determine the specific areas that will assist her in reaching her goals while outlining her skill barriers that must be improved as she moves forward.

Elisha also needs an opportunity to practice multiple times each week and to receive systematic feedback from an expert—her coach. She needs to follow the curriculum and receive suggestions, corrections, and encouragement on her efforts. If she is not putting her weight on the correct foot, then her coach needs to point that out. If she is dropping her guarding arm, then she needs to be reminded to focus on that arm. When she hits the bag with power or blocks a punch effectively, Elisha's coach needs to reinforce her correct technique. That systematic coaching will steadily enable Elisha to add and refine new skills on the way to her ultimate goal.

During the process, she will also need to reach benchmarks. Elisha's goal is to attain her black belt in two years. Along the way, she needs to know if she is on pace to meet that goal. The study of martial arts includes a preset system of benchmarking. Potential black belts are tested periodically to see if they earn the next belt color.

She may go from a white belt, to a yellow belt to a green belt and so on until she reaches a black belt. If she does not earn those various rankings in a specific timeframe, then she will not be on target to earn her black belt in two years. That progress monitoring will inform her workouts. If she is on target and earns those belts as expected, then she should stay the course. If she loses momentum and fails to keep on pace, then she will need to accelerate her training activities to get back on track.

It is easy to assume that Elisha will learn all of her new skills from her coach. Relying on one person to meet those needs, however, will not be sufficient. Her timeframe is very aggressive so she will have to maximize her learning. Therefore, Elisha needs to surround herself with other people who are committed to martial arts. In all likelihood, these folks will be pursuing the same goal at the martial arts studio. Some of her peers will be better than she and some will be worse. By participating with a cadre of similarly minded individuals, she will learn both formally and informally.

At times, she will receive explicit instruction from her peers. She may ask Ken to show her how he keeps his balance when he is completing the kicking combination. At other times, she will informally notice that Maria is using her entire body when she punches and that seems to be an effective technique. Elisha will then incorporate those techniques into her own practice. A group of athletes that are working toward the same goal all benefit from the brainstorming, modeling, motivation, and the element of competition that is present in any athletic pursuit.

Elisha also needs one last critical component to reach her goal. She needs to ensure that all of the resources in her life are aligned and focused on achieving this goal. She needs to determine that this is a major personal goal so that there cannot be other competing goals. This is not the time for her to pursue another college degree, for example.

Elisha also needs to recruit people in her life. As a wife and mother of three children, she needs to have some conversations with her husband and children to determine if this is a goal the family can help her pursue. Are all of the people in her life aligned to help her achieve her goal? Will her husband and children support her in taking the time it will require to meet her goal?

In summary, it is obvious that in order to change her "practices" to reach her goal, Elisha will need some very specific components for success. She will need:

- A clearly defined vision of her goal that is shared by her coach and herself. They need to know the specific skills she will need in order to be considered a black belt.
- A needs assessment that determines her starting point in terms of her physical strengths and weaknesses as related to martial arts.
- Engagement in a proven curriculum.
- Ongoing feedback and coaching from an expert.
- Formative assessments that will provide information so she and her coach can refine her training toward her end goal.
- Participation in a group of peers who are pursuing the same goal in order to formally and informally learn from each other.
- Alignment of the people and resources in her life to ensure they are all committed to helping her achieve her goal.

The original question was, "What does it take to change teachers' practices?" It actually takes the same elements to change teachers' practices as it takes to change Elisha's practices. Teachers need a clearly defined end goal for what instruction should look like in their classrooms. They need to specifically understand the components of GREAT instruction and what they will look like. They also need to receive ongoing coaching and feedback toward that improved instruction.

They need to review their progress against predesigned benchmarks. For teachers, that information will not only determine if their practices are improving over time, but also whether or not students are showing increased achievement. If students are not learning or if the teachers' practices are not improving sufficiently, then it is clear that the training and support provided to the educators must be improved to get both the teachers and students back on track.

Educators need to work with their colleagues, other teachers, and administrators who are working toward the end goal of improving instruction. They need to benefit from each others' experiences, expertise, brainstorming, and problem solving. They need to be engaged in conversations about the instructional elements implemented and their effectiveness for student learning. They need to continually brainstorm with others and observe their colleagues as they work toward refined instructional strategies.

They also need to benefit from aligned resources. All of the personnel in the school, particularly the leaders, instructional coaches, and external supporters, need to be aligned in working toward the same end goal of improved instructional practices. They all must have the same clear vision of what effective instruction should look like in every classroom. Any feedback the teacher receives should be consistent regardless of the specific person who is providing feedback. Coaches, administrators, and other leaders must have carefully defined the critical elements to be observed so they are all looking for the same observable practices. That way, the school will move efficiently toward the same clear end goal.

The job of school leaders, therefore, is to create systems of support, professional development, and leadership (as seen in the martial arts example) that enable teachers to steadily and systematically move their skills toward GREAT instruction. Leaders must build and implement:

- A clear and consistent vision of the expectations for GREAT instruction in every classroom.
- A needs assessment, or data analysis, to determine the starting point for every school year.
- A system of professional development activities that systematically moves teachers toward GREAT instruction.

- Mechanisms to provide ongoing feedback and coaching to teachers utilizing all members of the school leadership team.
- A system of progress monitoring to ensure that teachers are gradually improving their classroom practices and that students' learning is on track to meet curricular expectations.
- Structures so that teachers have the opportunity to formally and informally learn from each other as they work toward implementing GREAT instruction.
- Personnel and financial resources that are aligned and focused on GREAT instruction, with minimal distractions and interference.

How does this approach to changing adult practices compare to the "professional development" activities usually provided to teachers? Do schools typically provide the type of systematic support, coaching, leadership, and alignment that was described in the martial arts illustration? Unfortunately, most schools do not operate in this way. Teachers usually participate in a variety of one-shot training activities throughout the school year that are not usually aligned to one another.

During preplanning days at the beginning of the school year, they may get a brief overview of one instructional strategy. During the initial months of school, teachers will participate in various activities that do not necessarily provide follow-up to the previous training, but instead, compete with newer initiatives. As the year progresses, even more sporadic professional development experiences are layered upon those initial activities.

In addition, many schools have different expectations placed on teachers by different entities within the school system. The math department from the central office espouses one set of expectations while the special education department has different priorities. School leaders are responsible for coordinating all of these efforts while themselves adding their own expectations. A clear vision of what is expected has not been established by members of the leadership team or by the teachers themselves.

Therefore, teachers are responsible for somehow pulling in the variety of expectations and the content of numerous misaligned professional development initiatives and expectations to build a cohesive instructional program. In the end, this scattered approach to improving teachers' practices leads to more ineffective practices or a disregard for all new initiatives. In many schools, the efforts to improve student achievement resemble the hypothetical scenario in the industrial kitchen much more than the example in the martial arts studio.

Our challenge as educational leaders is to overcome these difficulties and align all central office administrators, school-based leaders, internal coaches, teacher leaders, teachers, and external supporters to build aligned systems so that teachers across the school implement improved instructional practices with fidelity. As leaders, we must develop a clear vision of what instruction should look like in every class and provide all of the elements of effective and efficient professional development systems.

The change in teachers' practices will ultimately result in students' showing radical improvement in student achievement. While we are building the efficient systems of change, we must also eliminate ineffective practices. We must weed out all of the inefficient activities that are routinely implemented in schools and are barriers to improved instructional practices. We must abandon activities that are not having a positive effect and replace them with activities that are streamlined, efficient, and ultimately have a positive impact on teachers' practices and student learning. Over the next few chapters school leaders will learn how to build efficient systems of change while bravely disregarding activities that clog their daily calendars and divert their attention.

QUESTIONS FOR REFLECTION

Chapter 3: Changing Adult Practices

1. Describe the professional development activities completed over the last two years in your school. Include all training programs, coaching exercises, and expectations placed on teachers to improve instruction. Are these efforts resulting in significant improvements in teacher practices and student achievement across your school? Over the last two years, has your school more resembled the cooking example or the martial arts example? Explain your answer.

2. If your school does not resemble the martial arts example, what effective components of improving educators' practices were missing and what ineffective activities were conducted?

4

✛

Aligning and Preparing
the Leadership Team

DATA ANALYSIS

As a school leader, how do you build ongoing direction and support for your faculty so that they provide GREAT instruction in the same way that the martial arts coach provides for novice athletes? It would be nice to think that the school principal can act in the exact same role as the martial arts coach and provide the majority of the ongoing coaching and feedback once a good system of professional development has been created. Unfortunately, the responsibilities of the principal are too broad to carry the load alone. In fact, none of the members of the leadership team have sufficient time to lead the charge in isolation.

The principal, assistant principal, instructional coaches, lead teachers, and external coaches all have a docket full of responsibilities. As individuals, they cannot provide the support and leadership that is required to change the practices of all teachers, but in combination they can certainly have the needed impact. The first step to changing teachers' practices across the school is to align every member of the leadership team so that they are prepared to build and implement intensive systems of support, coaching and leadership.

Initially, the members of the leadership team must conduct a needs assessment to determine the starting point for the school year.

This needs assessment must include an analysis of both quantitative and qualitative data over multiple years to help paint a complete picture of the school's strengths, weaknesses, and trends. This analysis should include a review of students' performance on statewide assessments over multiple years.

How are the students across the school performing in reading, English/language arts, science, written expression, and mathematics? In high schools, how are students performing on statewide assessments and in various courses? Over the last few years, has there been consistent progress in every content area or does the data indicate that there are subject areas in which the students are underperforming?

In addition to analyzing the performance of the entire student body, the leadership team should analyze the performance of each subgroup. Under the No Child Left Behind legislation, each subgroup much show sufficient progress in order for the school to make Adequate Yearly Progress. Are there subgroups of students who are underperforming?

Across the country, trends are emerging. Students with disabilities and students with limited English proficiency are lagging behind other subgroups in many schools and school districts. For years, these students were not included in school accountability systems. Now, schools must ensure that students in these subgroups, as well as other subgroups, are catching up so they can perform at higher levels like their peers. What about the performance of students from different ethnic groups? Are students from all ethnic groups performing at high levels or are there ethnic subgroups that are underserved?

When analyzing the performance of various subgroups, the leadership team should determine the causes behind the students' performance. For example, you might determine that students with disabilities are underperforming. It is appropriate to determine where the students are receiving their instruction. According to the United States Department of Education (2004), over 50 percent of students with disabilities spend at least 80 percent of their school day in general education classes. In your school, are there tendencies to educate students with disabilities in pull-out special education classes as opposed to general education classes?

Does data indicate that your school is educating more students with disabilities in pull-out, segregated classrooms when compared to the trends across the country? Should support systems be developed so that more students with disabilities can participate in general education classes successfully? Should steps be taken so that general education teachers provide differentiation and accommodations that will enable students with disabilities to be successful in their classes? Should professional development and support be provided to special education teachers so that they are equipped to support students with disabilities in general education classes?

When analyzing the performance of various ethnic groups, it is also effective to determine the causes of underperformance. Are some ethnic groups underperforming because there is a high rate of students with limited English proficiency in that subgroup, for example? According to A. Thernstrom & S. Thernstrom (2003), an analysis of the performance of Hispanic students indicates that students with limited English proficiency who are Hispanic exhibit lower levels of academic performance (as one might expect) than Hispanic students who are proficient in English. An analysis of achievement for Hispanic students indicates that as students become more proficient in English, that depressed performance largely disappears. This information is important as it will guide the leadership teams' actions. The interventions that are put in place would be different if a subgroup is underperforming due to students' need to master English rather than for other reasons.

The data analysis should also include a review of other factors such as rates of school attendance. Do students from across the school, or students within various subgroups, have higher than average rates of absenteeism? It is very difficult for students to learn the curriculum, to say the least, if they are not in school. If you determine that absenteeism is a problem, then it is appropriate to dig into the data to determine the cause of the absenteeism.

In some places, school leaders rely too heavily on school suspension as an intervention for inappropriate behavior. While suspending students may be appropriate at times, it can also become a default mechanism that does not ultimately improve student behavior. Therefore, the leadership team may determine that absenteeism is having a negative impact on student achievement, but the problem is not primarily due to students and families choosing to miss school. Instead, the problem may be due to ineffective approaches used to improve student behavior.

The data analysis will look differently for elementary schools, middle schools, and high schools. Typically, achievement data is more available for elementary students. A state test or norm-referenced test may be administered to students in every grade. Therefore, data can be compared across the school for each grade over multiple years. Data can also be analyzed across multiple years for each student to determine if the student is maintaining a certain pace of academic growth.

In middle schools, annual student achievement data will most likely be available as in the elementary schools, but other factors will gain in importance. In some school districts, student misbehavior spikes in middle schools. An analysis of discipline data will reveal what misbehaviors are prevalent across the school. That data can also be used to determine if there are specific times of the day, particular students, or specific locations that are high risk for misbehavior. You can also dig into data to determine if some students are becoming disenfranchised with school. Multi-faceted data analysis that includes class grades, absentee rates, discipline data, and teacher input might reveal middle school students who are high risk for dropping out of school once they reach high school.

In high schools, the data analysis may be more challenging as many high schools do not administer annual assessments of student achievement. In this scenario, a variety of data sources may need to be analyzed. This may include assessments that are given at the end of specific courses in high school, annual assessments from middle school, absentee rates, etc. High school is also a good time to analyze students' involvement in extracurricular activities. Students who fail to become involved in extracurricular activities may be at high-risk for academic failure and dropping out of school.

In high school, the data analysis at the student level will look like a profile. Once that profile is completed for each child, then students can be grouped into three groups, the red group, yellow group, and green group. The green group is moving along well and needs no additional support. The yellow group requires caution and a certain level of support. The red group requires the school leaders and teachers to stop and develop plans for support.

Why should a leadership team devote time to conducting a data analysis? This information will set the foundation for continued actions. As the leadership team reviews the different elements of GREAT instruction, the results of the data analysis will inform their work. If the data indicate that students are underperforming in mathematics but are being successful in other content areas, then the leadership team will focus their attention on the components of

GREAT instruction as they relate to mathematics. If science is an area of weakness for a particular subgroup, then the leadership team should analyze the elements of GREAT instruction for the specific subgroup in the context of science.

COMMON EXPECTATIONS

Once the data analysis is complete, the leadership team must have a consistent and clear vision of what is expected in every classroom. The martial arts coach must have a clear vision of the competencies of a black belt just like the school leadership team must specifically envision the expectations for GREAT instruction across the school. Earlier in the book, the following question was posed, "If you asked every teacher in your school what constitutes GREAT instruction, how many answers would you get?" In many schools, there would be a different answer provided by every teacher in the building.

Unfortunately, the same is true for every leader in the building. The principal might have a different expectation for GREAT instruction than does the assistant principal or the instructional coach or the department chairs. How can the faculty clearly understand the expectations for their classroom if the definition of GREAT instruction can be so loosely interpreted? How will the teachers move toward GREAT instruction, or even understand it, if each leader in the school espouses different requirements and expectations?

Even worse, many school leadership teams do not define any expectations for classroom instruction. They may require superficial components to be seen, such as the curricular objectives being posted in each classroom, but beyond that they frequently do not explicitly state what is required and expected instructionally across the school. In that scenario, teachers are left to themselves to implement their version of GREAT instruction, which in many instances is ineffective. Did the martial arts expert allow each new student to identify what skills are needed to earn a black belt? Of course not.

The principal, assistant principal, instructional coaches, lead teachers from general education and special education, department chairs, and external facilitators (regardless of their specific title in the school) must have a clear, *consistent*, and specific vision of what GREAT instruction should look like in every classroom in the school. What are the observable components of GREAT instruction that should be evident in every classroom regardless of the grade or the subject that is taught?

Once the leaders have a clear and consistent expectation for the school, then they can systematically lead all members of the faculty toward those expectations. In a previous chapter, a summary was provided of each element of GREAT instruction. In this chapter, specific, observable actions that the school leaders can expect to see will be described.

SPECIFIC CLASSROOM EXPECTATIONS—
GUIDED BY THE CURRICULUM

In order to ensure that the instruction is guided toward the curriculum expectations, the first component of GREAT instruction, the members of this group must be extremely familiar with the curriculum. In years past, it may have been acceptable for the leaders to relegate knowledge of the curriculum solely to their teachers, particularly in high school. That is no longer sufficient.

The leadership team must have expertise in the curriculum. That does not mean that every member of the leadership team should have knowledge about every subject area, but across the team there should be expertise in every subject that is taught in the school. They should have a very clear understanding of what students are expected to know and be able to do at the end of the school year and at various intervals along the way.

If a member of the leadership team were to observe a third grade mathematics class, he/she should be able to determine if the teacher is engaging students in the curriculum and is conducting activities with sufficient clarity, complexity, and sophistication. It is not enough that the curricular objective be posted in every classroom. Teachers must provide instruction that will enable the students to meet the curriculum expectations.

School leaders need to have a thorough understanding of the curriculum and be able to determine if the instruction provided in the class is clearly aligned and efficient in assisting students to achieve the curricular expectations. When observing students during their first semester of algebra, for example, the members of the leadership team should be able to tell if the students are engaged in the curriculum and on track to master the expected skills by the end of the first semester. If the leadership team as a combined unit does not have sufficient knowledge of the curriculum in every subject taught in the school, then they should expand the members of the leadership team.

That does not mean it is necessary, or even possible, to hire additional staff members. You will have to enlist members of your faculty who are experts in the needed areas to be working members of the team. In many instances, this will require partnerships with teacher leaders who have expertise in the content area. Their addition to the team will serve two purposes. They will add the needed expertise in the respective curriculum area.

They will also pave the way to ultimately improve teacher practices. Once the leadership team is aligned and turns its attention to supporting and coaching teachers throughout the school, then the involvement of the teacher leaders on the leadership team will reduce the likelihood that there will be significant resistance from teachers across the school. In fact, the teacher leaders who are chosen should be those who are respected by the faculty. Their credibility will build support from the teachers as GREAT instruction is expected and implemented across the school.

If your leadership team still does not have expertise in all content areas (even after recruiting teachers), then you might have to recruit individuals from outside of the school. In a previous chapter, we mentioned recruiting at least one individual from the central office to participate on your leadership team. When choosing that person, select someone who is an expert in the content area that your leadership team is missing. That way, that individual will not only represent the central office, but will also bring their content knowledge to the table.

SPECIFIC CLASSROOM EXPECTATIONS—RIGOROUS WITH RESEARCH-BASED STRATEGIES

One of the most common barriers to GREAT instruction is the lack of rigor. Teachers often speak of asking students to use higher-order thinking skills, but in actuality there are many teachers who do not routinely provide activities that will ensure that students become sophisticated problem solvers. This lack of rigor is often seen in middle and high school math classes.

At the beginning of the class, it is very common to see the math teacher ask the students to pull out their homework for a review. The teacher then ensures that students completed their homework and then he/she demonstrates select problems for the class. The students are primarily responsible for determining which problems they got correct. How can this activity be adapted to significantly increase rigor?

Before the students come into class, the teacher can post three different homework problems on each of the four walls of the classroom. The teacher will have intentionally completed those problems incorrectly. He/she will show all work. In four groups, the students should be asked to review the completed problems and determine "why" the problem is incorrect. Then, each group will write a paragraph about each problem that explains how the teacher arrived at the incorrect answer and what steps should be taken to correct the problem.

By using this approach, the common process of reviewing homework becomes a rigorous activity in which students have to analyze their teacher's work, compare it to their own homework, and determine the incorrect procedures that were used by the teacher. Some examples will include errors in calculation while other problems, particularly word problems, will include errors in how the teacher approached the problem. This simple activity takes ordinary instruction and turns it into rigorous instruction that will enable students to become sophisticated problem solvers.

Middle and high school English teachers can also increase their use of rigorous instruction. Students are often asked to read a narrative selection and answer literal and inferential questions in writing. That common activity can be ramped up with rigor. After reading *The Color Purple*, for example, students can be asked to answer comprehension questions in cooperative groups in stations around the room. At each station, students are presented with questions that require them to synthesize the motives, actions, and characteristics of the main characters of the story with present-day activities. For example, the following questions may be placed at each station.

- In the upcoming election, who would Celie vote for? Why?
- There is new legislation that requires small business owners to provide health insurance for their employees. Celie now owns

a business that has 5 employees. Is she in favor of or against this legislation? Why?

- This school district has just established separate schools for boys and girls. Is Celie in favor or against this initiative? Why?

At each station, the same questions should be asked, but from the perspective of a different character. At one station, identical questions will be asked from the perspective of Mister while at another table the same questions are posed from Shug's perspective. The students must work in their cooperative group to answer the questions at their station, then at a specified time, the students shift to the next station until they have answered three groups of questions. The teacher will then bring all groups together to debrief on their findings.

The teacher should not allow answers that are too simplistic. For example, students should not be allowed to choose a candidate (from the first question) based on his/her gender, ethnicity, or his/her home state. Students must dig deeper and develop opinions based on deep understandings of the character in the narrative and the current scenarios. This is another example of how routine instructional activities, in this case reading comprehension, can be altered to increase rigor and enable students to become sophisticated learners.

Research-based Strategies

The leadership team should also develop a list of research-based instructional strategies that should be seen at various times across the school. More importantly, they should agree upon what constitutes fidelity of the use of specific strategies. Many researchers suggest that effectively using visual organizers, for example, can increase students' academic skills. Most teachers will say that they use visual organizers effectively in their class when, in fact, many teachers do not.

Visual Organizers

Visual organizers can provide an excellent aid for organizing information. Teachers often lead students as they use word webs, for example, to structure information that they are attempting to learn. At the initial stages of using visual organizers, teachers will often provide the students with a graphic organizer style that will be most helpful given the particular topic that is being studied. One type of visual organizer might be used for information in a history class that reflects different events that occurred at different times whereas a different visual organizer might be used when the content contains new vocabulary words.

Many teachers stop there which limits the positive impact that can be gained from the use of visual organizers. As students become more competent in using visual organizers, teachers should reduce their prompting so that students are eventually able to construct visual organizers that summarize important components of the content and clearly demonstrate and simplify the sometimes complex relationships between the components. A student who is adept at creating and using visual organizers can demonstrate advanced levels of learning and will be able to start with a blank page, and unify information from a variety of sources and contexts to represent a coherent message.

A high school student in a U.S. History class, for example, should be able to synthesize information about the Civil Rights movement from a variety of sources (textbooks, visiting speakers, research, visual arts, government documents, legislation, etc.) to present recommendations to another country about how to move from a system of inequality in their country toward a system of equity. This visual organizer should pull together recommendations based on accomplishments in the Unites States, but also to help that country avoid ineffective strategies utilized in our country.

The student should be able to develop a visual organizer that is succinct and perhaps idiosyncratic in structure but conveys specific and sometimes complex messages in a clear and concise manner. In addition, the student should be able to explain and defend the content of the visual organizer so that an observer can understand the student's recommendations and the rationale for them. By utilizing visual organizers in this way, teachers will be providing rigorous and complex instruction and students will learn at deep levels.

Most students will not be able to begin using visual organizers in this manner. Teachers will need to introduce organizers in concrete and simple ways. Over time, teachers should eventually move students toward more independent and complex implementation. Ultimately, teachers will enable students to review all of the information that was presented over the last two weeks from a variety of sources and develop a one-page graphic organizer (starting with a blank page) that summarizes the most important components and clearly demonstrates how those components are interrelated.

After creating the visual organizer, each student should be expected to explain the information. In small groups, the teacher and the rest of the class can determine if the student was able to prioritize important information, exclude less important information, and summarize the relationships between all of the components.

If the leadership team determines that teachers across the school should be utilizing the research-based instructional strategy of visual organizers, then they should develop a consensus on what should be seen in every class. During the first several weeks of school, the team may expect to see teachers providing a variety of visual organizer structures for their students while students become more comfortable with their use.

By a specified time in the school year, the members of the leadership team should consistently expect to see the use of visual organizers with less prompting from the teacher. Perhaps students construct their own visual organizers when given a choice of structures and explain with some level of competence the ideas represented in the visual organizer. Over time, the leadership team should expect the prompts to fade while the students build sophisticated visual organizers. They should also see the students providing in-depth explanations about their visual organizers and expect to see the teacher and other students providing feedback regarding the accuracy and depth of understanding portrayed in the visual organizer and also in the students' explanation.

A rubric can be developed not only to assist members of the leadership team as they conduct classroom observations, but also to be helpful to teachers as they analyze their own practices. By having a specific timeline and expectation for the instructional strategy, the members of the leadership team can observe in classrooms and compare the classroom instruction with the expectations for that point in the year. If teachers are not meeting the instructional expectations then the leadership team should provide some specific coaching and feedback to the teachers.

The leadership team should determine a few research-based instructional strategies that should be seen across the school and focus diligently on those strategies until they are demonstrated with fidelity across the school. It is preferable to focus on a few strategies in the first year and ensure that the faculty understands those strategies deeply and uses them with fidelity. Then, additional strategies can be added during subsequent school years.

Pursuing a few strategies deeply is preferable to providing introductory-level knowledge on many strategies. Therefore, it is critical that school leadership teams choose strategies that will have a big bang for the buck. They should choose strategies that will have an impressive impact on student achievement.

Vocabulary Instruction

It may be effective to focus on vocabulary development (which will actually include a variety of related strategies rather than a single strategy). Unfortunately, many people assume that vocabulary development is synonymous with learning specific terminology. That is one aspect of vocabulary development, but the larger context also includes increasing students' expressive and receptive language skills. We want all children to demonstrate an ever-increasing skillfulness at writing, reading, speaking, and listening to information from a variety of sources and contexts.

We want children to not only use and understand a wide variety of terms, but we also want them to use language (orally and in print) in various ways depending on the context. We want students to express themselves in elaborated and complex ways. We want students to be able to express subtle and nuanced differences when the situation calls for that. We want students to respond with different emphasis (i.e., emotionally) depending on the situation or the material that is presented.

Recent research indicates that all children do not come to school with the same foundation in vocabulary and language. According to Hart and Risley (1995), children from families from different socioeconomic strata have widely different language experiences before coming to school. In an average hour, for example, preschool children from families receiving welfare heard over 600 words in a typical hour, while the average child from a working class family heard over 1,200 words and the average child from a professional family heard over 2,100 words.

Therefore, the results of the study indicate that children from highest socio-economic strata heard almost 4 times as many words in a typical hour than did their least-advantaged peers. Hour upon hour of this type of discrepancy can assumedly have a significant impact on a child's developing language and vocabulary. It is apparent that vocabulary/language development is critical for all students, but can be especially important for some students. The need for schools to respond with effective instruction is heightened for many students as their ultimate academic success can depend in large part on the classroom instruction that is provided.

This importance on language also passes the common sense test. Strong students have long since learned that they have an advantage once they master the terminology, language, and vocabulary of a particular field. Many individuals who read this book may have figured this out in college. Those individuals who are often labeled as "good students" learned that as soon as they mastered the "lingo" of a particular professor or the terminology in a certain field of study, then they were half-way home in gaining proficiency.

In fact, a skillful student can often use terminology effectively (the "buzz" words) and trick the professor that they have more proficiency than they actually have. The fact that some students can outwit their professors with well-placed terminology demonstrates the power of vocabulary/language development!

Vocabulary/language development can be considered in two broad ways. First, students need a wide variety of interactions with as much language as possible. They need language-rich environments where they are engaged with using, investigating, playing with and seeking out new terminology and new uses of words that they already know. Classroom teachers need to convey a strong priority and emphasis on using novel words in speech and in written expression.

Students need practice in investigating new words that they encounter in discussion and speech. Teachers must create classroom processes and instruction in which children are seeking out, gathering, and experimenting with new terminology. When observing classrooms, the members of the school leadership team should see the investigation, manipulation, and interaction with terminology to be ever present in all classrooms.

In addition to creating processes and environment described above, students need explicit instruction in particular terminology that is related to the curricular expectations. In fact, since all students in a particular grade/subject will be pursuing the same curricular standards, common vocabulary lists should be created that relate to the standards.

Ideally, the school district should convene a group of experts in the various subject matters who establish vocabulary lists for each grade, content area, and course. The vocabulary terms should not be limited to terminology that is extremely idiosyncratic to a particular field. In addition to those terms, the lists should include words that have a variety of uses and applications, thereby increasing students' vocabulary across contexts.

This approach to specific vocabulary terminology seems to be more reliable than allowing each teacher to develop his/her own list of terms related to the curricular standards. The lists can certainly be expanded upon by each teacher as described in the earlier paragraphs. The school or district should also provide curriculum maps that demonstrate in the curriculum where the various vocabulary words should be taught during the instructional year. This information should pinpoint a rough schedule during the year when specific words should be initially addressed.

Once the timelines and terminology lists are established, specific vocabulary strategies, the explicit vocabulary instruction, should be outlined across the school. Unfortunately, vocabulary instruction in many schools and classrooms is limited to providing a list of new words to the students, requiring students to look up the words in the dictionary, re-writing their definition and then expecting them to write a sentence with those words. Relying solely on these activities will almost certainly ensure that students will not increase their vocabulary/language skills.

One explicit vocabulary strategy involves creating categories with terms and then developing categories from terms. Let's say that middle school students are studying an instructional unit that includes this partial list of terms: obsessive, excitedly, subtle, exasperation, sneaky, selected, drafted, and determined.

First, students should place the terms in student-developed groups. At first glance, there may be 4 different groups of terms. Because of their related meaning, students might pair the following words: (1) obsessive/determined, (2) subtle/sneaky, (3) abundant/excessive, and

(4) selected/drafted. These terms have similar meanings given a specific context. The students respectively label these groups: (1) extreme focus, (2) not being noticeable, (3) plenty, and (4) chosen.

Some students may develop different groups for these terms, which is not only acceptable but reinforced. In fact, student learning is maximized when the students discuss various groupings and provide their rationale for their choices. Their discussions and re-working groups deepen students' knowledge and use of the terms.

Next, students should develop categories from the words. This time, each term becomes the title for its own category. Therefore, students have to focus on the differences in the terms rather than their similarities. Under each word, they should write information like: the context in which the term is used, who might use the word, and properties that make the word unique. Under the term "abundant," a student might write the following phrases:

- Means that there is plenty
- More than expected
- It is a good thing
- Will make people happy
- Example: If there was lots of food at a party and everyone was happy.

Under the word "excessive," a student might write the following phrases:

- Means there is plenty
- Having too much
- It is a bad thing
- Will make people feel uncomfortable
- Example: A person talked too much and people didn't like being around him/her.

Notice that even though these words have similar meanings, their context is very different. One of the terms has a positive connotation while the other term has a negative connotation. Of course, there might be a context in which that does not stay true, but by and large this activity enables students to develop a deeper understanding of the words. These types of activities will also increase the likelihood that the terms will become a part of the student's lexicon.

Impact on the Leadership Team

The leadership team should determine which handful of research-based strategies should be seen across the school and should specify expectations for the use of those instructional strategies with fidelity. The leadership team should develop a schedule in which these strategies will be introduced to the staff so that they are not overwhelmed with several new instructional strategies at one time. As the year progresses, teachers across the school will become more competent in using the instructional strategies. The leadership team will be able to determine which teachers are progressing in the use of specific, research-based instructional strategies and which teachers need additional support and coaching to refine their skills.

SPECIFIC CLASSROOM EXPECTATIONS—ENGAGING AND EXCITING

The leadership team should also develop a consensus about the level of engagement that should be seen in every classroom. This element is much more difficult to define or describe. You know it when you see it. The leadership team might decide that the best way to determine how effectively teachers are engaging students is to obviously determine if all students are actively engaged. That seems self-evident. All students in a class should be engrossed in their work. That is not the same as expecting students to be compliant.

At times, an observer might go into a class and see all students sitting appropriately in their seat while the teacher provides a lecture on a science topic. Those students may be obedient and respectful, but they may not be engaged and engrossed in their work. They could be thinking about anything but the topic at hand. In some classes, students don't even try to hide the fact that they are not engaged. You may see students sleeping, passing notes, or being disrespectful. Some students, particularly in some high schools, are so bored that they disengage over time and become high risk for dropping out of school.

The expectation should not merely be that teachers should maintain an orderly classroom, but they should provide activities that pull the students into the work. Every student in every class should be routinely engrossed in their activities.

SPECIFIC CLASSROOM EXPECTATIONS—ASSESSED
CONTINUOUSLY TO GUIDE INSTRUCTION

The leadership team should also clearly define what type of ongoing assessments will be used across the school to guide instruction. Using formative assessments to guide instruction is not the sole responsibility of specific teachers. Ongoing data should be analyzed at the classroom level, but it should also be analyzed by the leadership team. In order for such data analysis to occur, formative assessments must go beyond classroom grades. In many cases, relatively simple assessments can be provided that compare students' work to the curriculum standards. These assessments can be adopted or they can be developed at the school.

It may be preferable for teachers who teach the same subject matter to use common assessments. For instance, all second grade math teachers in the school should use common assessments that allow them to compare their students' performance to students in other classes and to the curricular expectations. The same applies to all geometry teachers or British Literature teachers in high schools and all pre-algebra teachers in middle schools. In collaboration with classroom teachers, the leadership team should determine what instruments will be used for formative assessments.

Perhaps the teachers who teach the same subjects can get together and develop assessments that can be used throughout the school year. According to O'Connor and Williams (2006), there are some positive outcomes when teachers collaborate to analyze the curriculum and develop common assessments. This process, in and of itself, will strengthen the teachers' understanding and expertise with the curriculum. The meaningful conversations between the teachers about the assessments and what types of questions and problems truly evaluate the standards of the curriculum will sharpen the teachers' skillfulness with the specific standards and thereby pave the way for more efficient instruction.

These mutual and collaborative activities between teachers are as beneficial to them as they are to the martial arts students who work together to gain their black belts. The teachers will learn from each others' perspectives and skills as they develop common assessments just as the martial arts students formally and informally learn from each other.

Regardless of the types of formative assessments that will be used, whether they are Curriculum Based Measurements as discussed in the previous chapter or common assessments that are developed at the school, the leadership team should determine the schedule for the administration of those assessments and how the results will be analyzed to impact instruction. The leadership team may determine that formative assessment data will be reviewed every three weeks. At that point, the data will be reviewed at two levels.

First, the leadership team should review the data. They should look at the data across: the school, subject areas, and teachers. They should determine if there are specific subject areas, grade levels, or teachers who need additional assistance. The student data will highlight patterns of weaknesses.

This phase of analysis is often skipped. Administrators will often rely on teachers to analyze formative data without analyzing it themselves. This is problematic. The leadership team has the perspective to provide a birds eye view of the data to spot trends across the school.

Then, teacher teams should analyze the data for their students while receiving facilitation by a member of the leadership team. Trends that were spotted by the leadership team will be shared. In addition, teachers will discuss specific elements that have contributed to the students' performance (both good and bad.) Those conversations then shift into discussions about how to adjust instruction in the future. Through this continual analysis of student growth (at both the leadership and teacher levels), instruction will become much more responsive to student needs.

A member of the school leadership team should be able to say to a teacher, "Show me which students in your class are exhibiting difficulty as seen on the formative assessments and describe the specific instructional strategies that will be implemented for those students over the next three weeks." In addition, the members of the leadership team can ask about the 20% of students who are doing very well and how those students will be given additional challenges to ensure that they learn at even higher levels.

This will be a paradigm shift in many schools. For many years, school administrators have focused on looking at lesson plans in isolation of student progress. The principal or assistant principal requires teachers to submit their lesson plans for review and approval once a week to ensure that the teachers have planned effectively. According to Baron, the receipt and review of lesson plans should be replaced with the receipt and analysis of formative assessment data. Instead of reviewing the lesson plans, assistant principals and other school leaders should spend the time reviewing the results of formative assessments across the school (Baron, K. June 20, 2007, personal communication).

School leaders should determine if there are trends that need addressing. They should determine if teachers and students are progressing satisfactorily and, if not, how instruction will be adjusted for those students. They should determine which students are exceeding expectations and ensure that instruction is responding to their needs for increased rigor.

In addition to focusing on the student performance, the analysis of formative data can also assist in determining if there are teachers who are struggling and need additional support to ensure that their students meet or exceed expectations. If large numbers of students in a given teachers' class are failing to meet the standard of competency on formative assessments, then the leadership team should determine the most effective ways to increase support for that teacher.

SPECIFIC CLASSROOM EXPECTATIONS—TAILORED THROUGH FLEXIBLE GROUPING

In addition to developing a specific plan and expectations for formative assessments, the leadership team should determine the specific expectations for the utilization of flexible groupings across the school. When team members observe instruction in a classroom, what specific use of flexible grouping should they expect to see? The obvious answer is that flexible groups should be completely aligned with the results of the formative assessments.

Teachers should have a specific rationale for the grouping patterns. At times, they will utilize homogenous groups in which all students in a particular group need similar instruction. At other times, teachers will utilize heterogeneous grouping patterns in which students have different instructional needs that can be met in the same group.

Once groups are established based on formative data, they may take the form of cooperative learning groups especially as students move toward upper elementary, middle, and high school. If used effectively, cooperative groups can increase student achievement.

Unfortunately, in many situations these groups are implemented poorly. In many classes, teachers will separate students into small groups for a quick activity or for an assignment. When provided this scenario, the students often break apart the task and give the various members of the group specific components. Later, they combine their various components into a whole.

The problem with this type of jigsawing is that none of the students gets a comprehensive understanding of the activity. Every student has a small portion of the whole, rather than an entire understanding. When using jigsawing, teachers should make sure that the information is not so broken up that none of the students understand the material in a deep and complex way.

In other classrooms, cooperative groups are implemented poorly in another way. This problem is seen in classes from primary schools through Graduate Schools of Education. When the teacher (or in the case of Graduate Schools of Education, the professor) separates the class into small groups and gives them a series of questions or challenges to solve, one or two of the participants naturally dominates the conversation. At the end of the discussion, the teacher asks the group to select their speaker and summarize the discussions of the group.

The individuals who dominated the discussion are typically nominated by their group to share the thoughts of the group which in actuality are the thoughts of one or two individuals. In these cases, all of the students do not master the concepts. One or two of the students are making progress, but the other students are merely passing the time. There is an easy way to overcome this problem. When the students are originally given the problems or questions to solve, the teacher should inform the class that he/she will choose the person who summarizes the group's discussions. This person will not be chosen until the cooperative activity is completed.

This encourages two desirable outcomes. First, all of the students will become engaged in the cooperative group discussions because any of the individuals may be called to represent their group. In addition, the students will feel responsible for preparing each other for the debriefing. The teacher will hear the students make statements to each other like, "Ask me the questions to make sure I answer them correctly." A higher percentage of the students will become proficient in the content.

If the members of the leadership team determine that cooperative groups can be an effective use of flexible groups, then they should come to a consensus on how that strategy should be used. They may determine that jigsawing can be used, but should be used so that all of the students gain a complete picture of the particular concept and are able to discuss the relationships between the various subcomponents. They may also determine that teachers should select which students summarize the cooperative group discussions just prior to the debriefing.

Those are two observable components that each member of the leadership team should expect to see when cooperative groups are utilized. In addition, when observing cooperative groups, the members of the leadership team should determine if every student in the class is fully engaged in the activity. If some students are fading into the background while their classmates dominate the discussion or activity, then the instructional strategy should be modified to be more effective for all students.

Co-Teaching or Shared Teaching

In many schools, there is an ideal context to provide differentiated instruction through flexible grouping. In many classes, there are two adults who are working with the same class of students. Special education teachers are often co-teaching with general education for a class of students that include students with and without disabilities. Teachers of students who are English language learners often share teaching responsibilities with general education teachers. Paraprofessionals are also supporting the instruction activities in many classrooms, especially in primary grades.

There has probably been more literature developed regarding co-teaching with general education and special education teachers than any other teacher pairs. According to Burrello, Burrello, & Friend (1996), there are six models of special education/general education co-teaching that describe the configuration of the adults and students in the shared classroom. Those models are: Team Teaching, One Teach/One Observe, One Teach/One Circulate, Station Teaching, Alternative Teaching, and Parallel Teaching.

The first three describe when whole-group instruction is being provided to all of the students. The latter three models describe configurations in which the students are placed in flexible groups with each teacher leading one of the groups. In "Station Teaching," there are at least 3 groups of students around the room in which students are completing different instructional activities. One teacher supervises one of the groups while the other teacher supervises the second group. The third student group includes independent student activities. The students rotate between the various groups to complete all of the activities.

"Parallel Teaching" describes when the class is divided into two groups. Each teacher leads one of the groups and covers the same instructional material. "Alternative Teaching" describes the scenario in which one teacher leads a larger group of students and the other teacher supervises a smaller group of students. The students in the smaller group may include students who need targeted instruction like pre-teaching or remediation. Or, the group may include students who need additional challenges and rigor.

Villa, Thousand, & Nevin (2004) describe similar general education/special education co-teaching configurations using different terminology: "Supportive Teaching," "Parallel Teaching," "Complimentary Teaching," and "Team Teaching." Again, some of these models represent whole-group instruction while "Parallel Teaching" represents different approaches to dividing the students into small groups with each teacher supporting a different group.

Even though the descriptions of co-teaching models described above have been written to describe the pairing of a general-education teacher and a special-education teacher, the same principles can apply regardless of the roles and titles of the teachers. There are two critical points regarding scenarios when there are two adults in the room. First, both teachers should be actively teaching the entire instructional period. That way, the "teaching time" in one 60-minute instructional segment can be doubled to 120 minutes of instruction.

If it is obvious that one of the adults is dominating the instruction while the other adult merely drifts around the room and reminds students to stay on task, then the real benefit from the shared teacher arrangement will be lost. In co-teaching arrangements, regardless of the roles or titles of the adults, the members of the leadership team should see both teachers actively engaged in instruction and providing feedback to students.

This is also the ideal time to provide flexible, small group instruction. Even though some may argue that one beneficial model is when the two teachers collaborate to lead a whole group of students and by the virtue of their background and expertise, provide a well-rounded discussion, this author suggests that the real benefit comes when both teachers are responsible for leading a small group of students. There are two different concepts that are almost irrefutable in the field of education. Students learn quicker and more solidly when they are provided more practice opportunities (more "turns") and are provided targeted feedback.

Small group instruction, when there are two adults in the room, provides an outstanding opportunity to provide that type of intensive practice and feedback. With a lower student to teacher ratio, each child in one teacher's small group will have the opportunity to have more attempts at practice (i.e., answering the teacher's question, reading a passage, or answering a mathematical problem) and to receive targeted feedback based on their attempt. The lower student/teacher ratio also allows for instruction that is tailored and differentiated based on each student's specific needs.

The grouping patterns of students with shared teachers follow the same principles as when there is only one adult in the room. The formation of groups should be based on ongoing, formative data. At times the groups will be homogenous while at other times heterogeneous groups will be implemented. In the two-teacher classroom, care should be taken to ensure that students are not segregated into groups based on a particular categorization. There should not be groups solely comprised of students with disabilities or students who are English language learners, for example.

Developing a Consensus for the Leadership Team

The leadership team should develop a common consensus on what should be seen in classrooms with one teacher and those classrooms with two adults. All teachers should be routinely differentiating instruction using flexible groups based on ongoing assessment data. This should be an expectation for all classrooms. For classes with two teachers, the expectation should be that both teachers are actively teaching the entire instructional segment and the majority of the instruction is provided in flexible groups with each teacher leading a separate group of students.

ALIGN ALL PROGRAMS AND INITIATIVES
TOWARD GREAT INSTRUCTION

Once the leadership team has a consistent understanding of each element of GREAT instruction, the next step toward ultimately improving teacher practices is to align all of the initiatives and programs in the school toward GREAT instruction. Schools are responsible for providing varied programs and services for different students.

There are special education programs for students with disabilities, Title I programs for students who are designated as economically disadvantaged, and Title III programs for students who are English language learners for example. In addition to those Title programs and others, schools implement new textbook series almost annually for different subjects.

There are also different initiatives that come from the school district or the State Department of Education. There are new curriculum standards, new school-wide behavioral approaches, and new instructional expectations. Many of these activities are supported with different funding sources so that implementation and bookkeeping for specific efforts can become isolated from the rest of the school.

The problem with these layers of initiatives is the negative impact that they have on teachers throughout the school. Because of the various expectations and requirements for the different activities, it is easy for classroom teachers, and the school leaders for that matter, to feel that all of their efforts are disconnected and ultimately for cross purposes. The various recordkeeping activities that teachers are asked to complete and the varied instructional activities that they implement seem in competition with one another. The classroom practices suffer from a lack of clear focus.

In order to successfully change teachers' practices so that they are able to implement GREAT instruction, the leadership team must make sense of all of the swirling activities and expectations. This process is easier than one might expect. At the core of each of these initiatives and programs is instruction. Ultimately, they are all about or can be shaped to support the vision of GREAT instruction. The Title programs, for example, are moved forward with GREAT instruction. All subgroups of students, including those with disabilities, those from economically disadvantaged circumstances, and those students who are English language learners, to name a few, will benefit from each element of GREAT instruction.

The same can be said for new textbook adoptions or new instructional initiatives promoted by the school district or the State Department of Education. They can all be centered on implementing GREAT instruction. The problem is that leadership teams do not see the commonalities between the various expectations. Therefore, teachers cannot see that their efforts can be streamlined and aligned.

It is imperative that the leadership team align all of the initiatives and communicate them to their staff so that they see them as different elements of the same purpose. The various activities must be hung on the existing structure of GREAT instruction. If the school district adopts a new textbook series in math, then the leadership team demonstrates to the math teachers how the series includes formative assessments that are a component of GREAT instruction, aligns in part to the state-directed curriculum, allows for the use of research-based strategies, and fosters the efforts to provide rigorous instruction to the students. The leadership team should clearly explain that the new textbook series is one tool that will help them implement GREAT instruction. It is not something else that competes with existing efforts.

The same can be said for the paperwork and activities that are required for special education services. According to the Individuals with Disabilities Education Act (2004), an Individual Education Program (IEP) must be developed for every child who has a disability and participates in special education and related services. It includes a description of impact that the disability has on the student's educational efforts, specific goals that will be addressed at school, and the special education and related services that will be provided to the student.

The IEP can easily become a voluminous document. The leadership team must demonstrate how the process of developing the IEP contributes toward providing GREAT instruction. The IEP goals for each student, for example, should assist the student in achieving the curricular expectations. In many cases, the assessments noted on the IEP should be the same as the formative assessments that are used to guide continued instruction, a vital component of GREAT instruction. According to O'Connor and Williams (2006), an IEP, once developed, should enable a child to meet or exceed expectations on the statewide assessments. If a student's IEP does not sufficiently describe actions that will enable the student to meet or exceed expectations, then the IEP should be re-worked.

This type of alignment and continuity can be established for almost all activities, programs, and initiatives that enter a school. It is the job of the leadership team to reshape and connect each of those efforts for the faculty so that they support the momentum to provide GREAT instruction rather than being an unrelated effort that competes with GREAT instruction.

It takes a tremendous amount of insight and determination to clearly align and communicate this type of streamlining for your staff. Unfortunately, many leaders are not able to align their initiatives within their building, and they are somewhat overwhelmed by the various competing expectations. These expectations are not likely to go away, but the effective principal must be willing to make sense for his/her staff of all of the various initiatives and programs that are required of the school.

In an effort to align the various initiatives and programs, school leadership teams must be willing to re-shape information that is shared with the school staff. As the various expectations are shared with the Title providers, the special education staff, and the teachers of students who are English language learners, for example, school leaders should help link the initiatives so that all members of the faculty and staff see how they are connected and directed toward improving instruction and learning for all students in the school.

This does not mean that leaders should try to filter information. In this day and age of complete information access, trying to filter information would be seen as manipulative and would create distrust in the school building. Instead, school leaders should re-shape information so that the faculty and staff can envision how the various initiatives are related. Leaders should stress their commonalities about instruction rather than the processes that differentiate the initiatives and programs.

Central office personnel also have a role in the alignment of the various programs and initiatives. Because of the mere size of the various Title programs, for example, different departments within the central office may manage the implementation of Title I from Title III. With the various departments, it is easy for the multitude of initiatives to seem extremely unrelated to one another once they make their way to the schools. Central office personnel should make a concerted effort to align and streamline their efforts and activities so that they arrive at schools seemingly more connected.

QUESTIONS FOR REFLECTION

Chapter 4: Aligning and Preparing the Leadership Team

1. Does your leadership team include expertise in all content areas that are taught in your school? If not, who will you add to your team?

2. How will your team ensure that the teachers in your school are guided by the curriculum? What specific indicators will you expect to see in classrooms that will indicate that instruction is aligned to the curricular expectations? Your answers should go beyond the expectation that teachers should post the curriculum standards that are being addressed.

3. As a leadership team, how will you ensure that teachers are providing sufficient rigor in their instruction? What specific teacher practices and student activities will you expect to see in classrooms? The answers should include a description of the type of student performance that will indicate that students are becoming sophisticated learners.

4. Who in your school district will you rely on to analyze the available research and succinctly summarize that research for consideration from your staff? How will that information be shared so that it is complete, succinct, and understandable? How will you make sure that the information provides a summary of how the specific instructional strategy should be implemented with fidelity?

5. Describe three to four specific research-based instructional strategies that will be implemented across your school. Describe the specific components that should be seen when these instructional strategies are utilized. What specific expectations do you have for the implementation of those instructional strategies? Describe the timeline that will be implemented so that various instructional strategies will be introduced and supported systematically throughout the year.

6. When conducting classroom observations, what will the members of the leadership team look for to determine if

students are sufficiently engaged and excited by their class activities?

7. Describe the formative assessments that will be implemented across grade levels/subject areas to gauge student's progress toward the curricular expectations. Will the school utilize Curriculum Based Measures, for example, and/or will teachers develop common assessments that will be used among teachers who are teaching the same content area?

8. Describe the process that the leadership team, in collaboration with teachers, will use to review the results of formative assessments. How often will those results be reviewed and how will the leadership team provide direction and support to teachers based on those results?

9. As the leadership team, what expectations do you have for teachers to utilize flexible groups as a component of their daily instruction? How often do you expect to see small group instruction in teachers' classrooms and how will you determine if the flexible grouping patterns are established based on ongoing formative assessments?

10. Describe the expectations that you will have for co-teaching teams in your building (regardless of the adults' particular job title). What expectations will you have for each shared team to utilize flexible group instruction to differentiate for students' individual needs?

11. As the leadership team, how will you align all initiatives and programs within the school so that they converge in a unified effort to providing GREAT instruction? How will you center all activities (i.e., special education programs, Title programs, foreign language activities, math instruction, and services for English language learners) on the concepts of GREAT instruction? How will you unite all professionals in the building, regardless of their specific job title or activities, so that they are all united around providing GREAT instruction?

5

Equipping Teachers to Provide GREAT Instruction

The first step toward implementing GREAT instruction in every class across the school is to align all of the school's leaders so that they have a common and clear vision of GREAT instruction. The second step is to align all of the various school initiatives and programs toward systematically improving instruction. Those two components prepare and equip the leadership team to lead the troops effectively. This type of alignment and unity among all of the school leaders establishes an extremely strong foundation for the next phase of activities, which involves systematically changing the practices of every teacher in the school.

It would be ineffective to gather all of the school's teachers in a faculty meeting and declare that the school will now be implementing GREAT instruction in every classroom. Merely announcing new expectations, no matter how clever or engaging the professional development activity, is not sufficient to improve teachers' practices in a systematic and reliable manner. As mentioned in an earlier chapter, learning new skills takes time, effort, and practice. Teachers need the opportunity to try out new skills and work together to refine those skills until they are able to implement better practices with fidelity and effectiveness.

The purpose of this chapter is to describe a process for systematically moving toward more effective practices. Instead of merely announcing and then expecting improved practices, a specific sequence of activities will be described that, if implemented, will provide a supportive structure so that all teachers can gradually and effectively move toward GREAT instruction.

IMPLEMENT FORMATIVE ASSESSMENTS

In chapter 4, a description was provided of the specific decisions the leadership team should make as they specify each component of GREAT instruction. In order to maximize efficiency, the team should implement those decisions in a very specific sequence. The first activity should be to implement the formative assessments that were decided upon by the members of the leadership team (that included teacher leaders).

During the first few weeks of school, the formative assessments should be established for all courses for the entire school year. The only exception may be in a school in which the teachers teach all content areas. This situation may be seen in kindergarten through third grade where the teachers teach all subjects. In that situation, it may be overwhelming to introduce all formative assessments during the first weeks of school during the same school year. One or two of the subject areas can be delayed until midway during the school year so that the teachers are not overwhelmed.

There is power in teacher teams developing their own common formative assessments. Whether or not teachers develop them, in order to implement formative assessments, teachers must have a copy of them and have been trained on their administration. The members of the school leadership team should discuss when each of the formative assessments will be given and how the results of the assessments will be used to guide instruction.

Minimally, the formative assessments should be administered at least every three weeks and the results analyzed as quickly as possible after administration. The goal with formative assessments is to get the biggest bang for the buck. Ideally, the formative assessments will require minimal time for the teacher and students while providing optimal information for determining if students are making sufficient progress toward curricular expectations.

Once teachers are equipped with the formative assessments, many teachers will naturally shape their instruction so that curricular standards are addressed in the classroom. So even before the first formative assessment is administered, they will have an impact on classroom instruction.

UTILIZING TEACHER TEAMS TO ANALYZE FORMATIVE ASSESSMENT RESULTS

As the formative assessments are being established, the leadership team should develop a process and a schedule for teams of teachers to meet to review the results of the formative assessments and brainstorm how those results should impact ongoing instruction. These meetings should occur after each administration of the formative assessments. They should be scheduled and identified as a top priority for the teachers. At least one member of the leadership team should facilitate each teacher group.

Traditionally, it has been common for teachers to have planned meetings to discuss student progress. Often, those meetings do not ultimately result in increased student achievement. First and foremost, the meetings must center around the discussion of the students' performance on the formative assessments. They should be structured so that teachers review students' progress on the assessment and use that information to shape continued instruction.

Teachers should discuss the students who are easily meeting the expectations on the formative assessments, and describe specifically how those students are performing in their classrooms. How are they demonstrating a deep understanding of the material? What explains the students' success? What should be done in upcoming instruction to continue to challenge them to meet high standards? Next, the teachers should discuss the students who are not meeting expectations on the assessments. Are there common threads across the students? Are they evidencing weaknesses in the same area? What kinds of errors or weaknesses have been observed in their work?

At subsequent formative assessment meetings, teachers should expand their discussions by reviewing how students responded to

the strategies discussed at the previous meeting and then implemented in the classroom. The flow of these discussions may proceed
in this manner:

- Each teacher reports on the students who achieved at higher
  levels as seen on the previous formative assessment. They
  should then briefly explain the strategies that were recommended at the previous meeting and the students' performance
  on the most recent formative assessment.
- Each teacher next reports on the students who did not meet expectations on the previous formative assessments. The teachers
  will briefly review the strategies that were recommended and
  report whether the students met expectations on the most recent formative assessment.
- Each teacher finally reports on any student who is new to either
  category: those students who exceeded or did not meet expectations on the most recent formative assessment. Instructional
  strategies will then be brainstormed.

By following this process, students who are exceeding, meeting, or
failing to meet expectations will be discussed regularly and systematically. By implementing these structures for formative assessment
reviews and ensuring that teachers make these meetings a priority,
the leadership team will enable teachers to benefit from each other's
expertise while successfully responding to student needs.

EXPANDING THE CONVERSATION—FLEXIBLE GROUPINGS

Once the teachers become accustomed to the routine of administering formative assessments and meeting in teacher groups (with ongoing direction from a member of the leadership team) to brainstorm instructional interventions systematically, it is time to expand
the discussion to include flexible groupings. At this point, teacher
groups should begin to discuss how flexible groups can be utilized
to respond to the results of the formative assessments.

This discussion should develop smoothly and naturally from existing conversations. In fact, many teachers will automatically discuss flexible grouping patterns that should be implemented when
they brainstorm instructional interventions. However, some teacher

teams will need to be prompted to include this approach in their discussions and practices.

Depending on the specific data and the instructional strategies utilized, a teacher may implement either homogenous or heterogeneous groups. A group of students who need specific instruction in a weak area may be brought together to work on those particular skills for a few days. Or, the groups could be heterogeneous and include students with a variety of skill levels. The groups should not be static, which could unintentionally establish negative tracking patterns for the students. By extending the formative assessment teacher groups to include the discussion of flexible grouping patterns, your teachers will add another element of GREAT instruction.

PROFESSIONAL DEVELOPMENT CONTINUED WITH EXPLICIT TRAINING

The teacher discussions described above can be an extremely beneficial facet of professional development. By focusing on the connection between continually refining instruction and its impact on student achievement, teachers will invariably improve their instructional practices.

This facet of professional development should be combined with explicit training in specific instructional strategies, monitoring, and peer observations. Members of the leadership team can provide this training since they previously determined the individual components of specific research-based instructional strategies that should be seen across the school. The training could also be provided by teachers in the school who are extremely competent in the instructional strategy. They may be ongoing members of the leadership team or be enlisted because of their facility in their classroom.

Training may occur during weeks in which the teachers do not meet to discuss formative assessments. For the first eight weeks of school, training activities may be provided every other week on utilizing visual organizers and implementing effective vocabulary instruction. By focusing on specific instructional strategies and providing trainers with multiple opportunities to provide information and teachers with a forum to share their experiences and ask questions, all of the teachers in the school will steadily improve their skills. In eight weeks or so, teachers will be implementing visual organizers as described earlier in this book.

During the first and second training session, various visual organizers may be introduced that match specific subject matter content. One type of visual organizer could be discussed as an effective way for students to organize information that includes historical facts. A different type of visual organizer may be presented as an effective way for students to organize two sides of a political argument. During these trainings, the trainer will share the ultimate expectations for the use of the instructional strategy for both teachers and their students.

The teachers will understand that they should steadily enable students to perform at deeper levels and should minimize their prompts. Students should be able to develop a visual organizer from a blank sheet of paper that connects the concepts that have been shared over multiple classroom activities. The students should also become competent in explaining their visual organizer, either verbally or in writing, so that their teachers and peers understand the complex relationships between the various components on the visual organizer.

The same process can be established for implementing effective vocabulary instruction. Therefore, the same training sessions (or subsequent training sessions) can be the context for providing explicit training and opportunities for discussion on the instructional components for effective vocabulary instruction, as agreed upon previously by the leadership team.

Even though a trainer may be leading these sessions, there should be a significant amount of time available for the teachers to work in small groups and discuss the implementation of the instructional strategy. These training sessions will probably not last more than one hour and ideally would occur during teachers' planning periods. In that way, the trainer's schedule includes leading small-group sessions all day during the same day. For some schools, the sessions may be even shorter as some elementary schools, for example, may be limited to a thirty-five minute planning period.

Teachers' planning time, however is not the only time when this training can occur. Some schools have a segment of time after the students leave and before the teachers' workday ends. That time may be utilized as long as the trainer is extremely engaging. He/she will have to be entertaining and dynamic to compete with the teachers' fatigue and distraction at the end of a long day.

As teachers become more proficient in the specific instructional strategy, the leadership team will introduce another instructional strategy. In the martial arts example, Elisha steadily became more proficient, in part, because her coach systematically introduced new skills that became building blocks for more skills. This same approach should be taken by school leaders. As teachers demonstrate proficiency in implementing one instructional strategy with fidelity, then another research-based strategy should be introduced in the training sessions and then reinforced in subsequent discussion groups.

MONITORING AND COACHING

Leaders must also provide follow-up support and monitoring in classrooms to ensure that all elements of GREAT instruction, including the research-based strategies, alignment with the curriculum, and the utilization of flexible groups, are being implemented effectively. Previously, the leadership team developed a common understanding of how the selected research-based strategies should be implemented in the school. This criterion for the implementation should be the driving component of the training provided to the teachers and it should also drive observations conducted in the classrooms.

The leadership team should compare teachers' practices with the criterion for implementing the instructional strategy. At some point following the observation, the individual from the leadership team who observed the teacher should provide feedback in a constructive and positive manner. This type of observation is not necessarily intended to be the official observation for personnel evaluation, but it should be similar to what is seen in that martial arts studio—an opportunity for a professional to provide feedback to a colleague.

In order for observational coaching to be effective, feedback needs to be provided on a regular basis. The problem is that school principals are inundated with responsibilities. It would be nice if they had a of couple hours every day to spend in classrooms, making observations and providing constructive feedback to teachers. That is not the case. The same can be said for all members of the leadership team: assistant principals, instructional coaches, lead teachers for special education, department chairs, other teacher leaders, and external support personnel.

However, each of those professionals does have some time to spend observing classrooms and providing consistent feedback. The leadership team should collaborate to develop a schedule in which each leader spends time observing teachers in classrooms and providing feedback. By combining efforts, they can devote a significant amount of time to providing classroom support and feedback.

This is where aligning the leadership team really pays off. If all members of the leadership team have a strong understanding and a clear consensus of the important characteristics of the selected instructional strategies and every element of GREAT instruction, then they will provide consistent feedback to all of the teachers in the building. Once teachers begin to hear the same type of expectations from every school leader, then momentum will build and teachers will move toward improving instruction with fidelity.

This alignment and persistent presence will also circumvent one of the barriers to school improvement that is seen in many schools. Teachers will be less likely to take the position that this new initiative is a passing fad that will quickly fade. Teachers will see that there are streamlined and focused expectations combined with the needed support, which will be in place for the long term.

In addition to the observations conducted by school leaders, teachers should be given the opportunity to spend time making peer observations. However, the purpose of peer observations is quite different than the observations provided by members of the leadership team. According to Showers and Joyce (1996), the purpose of peer observation is not to provide feedback to the teacher or to evaluate the effectiveness of instructional interventions, but to learn from the practices of other teachers. In fact, teachers should be discouraged from providing feedback. The observer, rather than the one who is observed, will benefit from the opportunity to see others implement their craft. These types of observations, coupled with the work of the teacher teams, can have a positive impact on teachers implementing new skills with fidelity and effectiveness.

SUMMARY—CHANGING TEACHER PRACTICES

The real challenge to radically improving student achievement is to build systems to steadily and systematically improve teacher practices with fidelity. Teachers need a structured system for improving their practices toward a well-defined end goal. Leadership team members will develop a consensus on specifically what each element of GREAT instruction should look like in their school. By creating that consensus, the leadership team will develop clear expectations for their faculty.

The next step, as discussed in the previous chapter, is to align all of the programs and initiatives in the school. They all focus on improving instruction, but it is easy to get lost in the details of each initiative and program and lose the focus on effective instruction. The leadership team should align each of those initiatives and programs so that teachers are able to see them as components of the same process to get to the same end—improving student achievement through GREAT instruction.

Once school personnel and initiative alignments are in place, school leaders should implement specific, concrete steps to improve the practices of their teachers over time. They should facilitate the selection or development of common formative assessments that can be used by teachers who teach the same subject, grade, or course. The formative assessments should be aligned to curricular expectations and should provide teachers with valuable information that can inform their continued instruction.

Once formative assessments are in place, the leadership team should schedule small-group teacher meetings in which the teachers share the results of the most recent formative assessments and discuss how those results inform continued instruction. These discussions should include the establishment of flexible groups to meet students' needs. These teacher groups should also discuss the instructional strategies that will be steadily and systematically implemented across the school.

In addition, explicit training activities should be provided by members of the leadership team to provide the faculty an opportunity to discuss the implementation of specific research-based instructional strategies. The members of the leadership team will also collaborate to provide classroom observations and constructive, positive feedback to the teachers. Even though each leadership-team member is unable to commit the necessary time to observations, their combined efforts can create a significant presence in classrooms. Finally, teachers need the opportunity to conduct peer observations, not for the purpose of evaluating their peers' practices, but for the purpose of being exposed to different colleagues implementing their craft.

This approach to changing teachers' practices may seem overwhelming, but over time it will seem natural and completely related to classroom instruction. Traditionally, schools have provided minimal support and intensity to improve the practices of teachers. Consequently, many instructional initiatives fall short of truly changing adult practices and student achievement. By implementing all of these complimentary steps, teachers will use and refine their practices with fidelity and students will demonstrate improved achievement.

QUESTIONS FOR REFLECTION

Chapter 5: Equipping Teachers to Provide GREAT Instruction

1. In your school, describe the formative assessments that will be used among teachers who teach common subjects, grades, or courses. What is the schedule for the administration of those assessments? (At a minimum, the formative assessments should be administered once every three weeks.)
2. Describe when small groups of teachers will meet to discuss the results of the formative assessments. Make a schedule for their meetings and assign at least one member of the leadership team to be an ongoing member of each teacher group.
3. Develop an agenda for the formative assessment teacher teams that will ensure that the teams discuss the performance and strategies for students who exceed expectations and those students who do not meet expectations. Provide an opportunity at consecutive meetings to discuss the progress that students have made as a result of the instructional interventions implemented.
4. Describe the schedule that will be used to provide explicit professional development activities for your teachers. Who will provide the training and which instructional strategies will be taught in what order?
5. Describe how members of the leadership team will conduct classroom observations. Assign each member of the leadership team to specific teachers for their observations.
6. Describe how teachers will be given the opportunity to conduct peer observations.

6

Build Tiers of Support for Struggling Students

When all teachers implement GREAT instruction, many more students will meet and exceed curricular expectations. All subgroups of students will perform at higher rates. In particular, students from subgroups that have traditionally underperformed will meet and exceed expectations. However, even with GREAT instruction implemented routinely, some students will experience difficulty meeting the standards.

Traditionally, schools have had two options for those students. First, schools rely on the creativity of each teacher to find and implement solutions in the classroom. The difficulty with this option is that it is extremely inefficient. If teachers in various classrooms across the school are independently starting from scratch to find solutions for children that have similar difficulties, then those teachers do not benefit from each other's work. Nor do they benefit from the experience of teachers who have solved the same types of difficulties for other students in previous years.

The other prevailing solution is to seek some type of special label for the student so that he/she can receive instructional services from another professional. In many cases teachers have sought to get a disability label for students so they can participate in special education services. Some students truly have a disability and should be afforded special education and related services to meet their unique needs. Other students, unfortunately, are inappropriately given a disability label when their real problem is that they have not had the opportunity to participate in intense instruction that enables them to catch up to their peers.

A TIER OF STANDARD INTERVENTIONS

In order to remedy the lack of options for students who struggle, schools should develop "standard intervention protocols" in which preset interventions are implemented in schools to respond to students who experience difficulty.

Standard Intervention for Struggling Algebra Students

In middle school and early high school, for example, many students have difficulty with algebra. Year after year, this course is the breaking point for many struggling students. Students enter without the prerequisite skills they will need to tackle the subject matter (even if the instruction includes all of the components of GREAT instruction).

Effective middle and high schools develop standing interventions for students who have trouble with algebra. This may take the form of an intensive tutorial course provided to students before they start algebra. Students could participate in a course that explicitly covers the fundamental skills of arithmetic and the vocabulary needed before they enter algebra. The success of this intervention will rely on the intensity of the instruction provided. Since these are students who have not acquired the necessary prerequisite skills, the instruction should be extremely systematic and taught explicitly.

Many schools implement activities they would consider to be a second tier of instruction for struggling students, perhaps even a minicourse like the one described here. The problem is that if you ask school leaders if the minicourse is successful, they respond with blank stares or with answers like, "Yes, many of our students learn a lot." That is not necessarily an objective evaluation of the effectiveness of the minicourse.

This type of answer tells you that the interventions being attempted may or may not be effective. The answer is truly unknown as school personnel are not determining if students who enter the algebra course after participating in this tier of interventions are more successful than other students who struggle, perhaps in previous semesters, and did not participate in the course. School personnel are also failing to determine if participating students are gaining skills they did not have prior to their participation in the minicourse.

Such courses or minicourses should include all of the components of GREAT instruction, and they should be more intense. There is greater responsibility that the instructional strategies be implemented with fidelity. There is a greater need to collect formative data to determine if the students are responding to instruction. Since these students have been less responsive to traditional instruction than other students, the instruction must be more intense, more exact, and more closely monitored.

Standard Intervention for Struggling Readers

Another example of an effective standard intervention protocol has been described by O'Connor, Primm, and Nanda (2008) that was designed as a standard intervention for first and second grade students who were not learning to read sufficiently. In this initiative, high school students tutored first and second grade students who were not learning to read at expected rates.

The high school students utilized the scripted Direct Instruction text, *Teach Your Child to Read in 100 Easy Lessons* (Englemann, Haddox, and Bruner 1983), which was originally designed for parents to use with their children. In this intervention high school students spent approximately thirty minutes a day with the youngsters at least four days a week. The tutorial activity did not replace the reading instruction that was provided to the students by their teacher, but instead was provided during another part of the school day to supplement that classroom instruction.

This initiative was implemented at three different elementary schools in Georgia across multiple years so there were actually eight different cohorts of participants and their tutors. The outcome data demonstrated that the eighty-three first and second graders spent an average of approximately six months in the tutorial program during which time their word identification grew by an average of nine months and their passage comprehension skills grew by one year and four months (rounded to the nearest month) according to the pre- and post-assessments conducted (Woodcock 1998).

The students' growth in standard scores (on the same assessment) was equally impressive. The students' average pretest scores in word identification and passage comprehension were 95.92 and 82.60 respectively, while their posttest standard scores were 104.94 and 103.28. On average, the students made significant growth in both word identification and passage comprehension.

This intervention, or standard intervention protocol, showed that students who were behind their peers in either reading comprehension, decoding, or both were able to gain ground when compared to their chronological age. They were able to make more progress in reading than the amount of time they spent in the tutorial program.

The research study also reported longitudinal information on the students, which was available for seventy-five of the original eighty-three students. The data on seventy-five students showed that four of the students were labeled as having a disability and received special education services either before or while they were in the tutoring program. Of the seventy-one students who finished the tutorial initiative and were not receiving special education services, only three were ultimately identified as having a disability.

Even though it is unclear how many of these students would have been labeled as having a disability if they had not participated in this intervention, it is probably safe to say that many of the students were at high risk of gaining a disability label since they were already falling behind their peers academically in first and second grade. This data also supports the likelihood that some students who are inappropriately labeled as having a disability may not be considered for a disability label if they receive intensive and systematic instruction when they first exhibit signs of falling behind.

The longitudinal data also showed success on the statewide assessment, the Criterion Referenced Competency Test (CRCT), which is used to determine if a school meets the state's accountability standards. In Georgia at the time, first and second grade students had to score 300 points on the CRCT to meet expectations or 350 to exceed expectations. The longitudinal data showed that the average score on the reading subtest of the CRCT after participation in the tutorial initiative was 332 points, far exceeding the standard to meet expectations.

This data reflected the students "most recent" CRCT score when the data was collected. Therefore, the CRCT scores were collected between one and three years after the tutorial project, depending on the particular student. This indicates that the gains made during the tutorial project were maintained, a pattern we don't often see for intensive services for young children.

This intervention was also effective for another reason. Remember that GREAT instruction must be engaging and exciting. The tutorial activities truly met that bar. It was incredible to see the big high school students interacting with the younger students. The first and second grade students looked with awe at the older students while the high school students received and returned that admiration. It was truly magic to see high school students work diligently with their young friends.

Building Standard Interventions

How does a school determine what types of interventions should be implemented for their students? School leaders should analyze a variety of data sets to determine the areas in which students have traditionally shown difficulty in their school.

A high school may determine that a high correlation exists between students who exhibit misbehaviors consistently and students who drop out of school. In that case, proactive interventions should be established for students who exhibit negative behavior. A middle school might discover a pattern that students have trouble with science. An elementary school might determine weaknesses are evident in mathematics.

This type of data analysis might reveal two things, one of which was discussed in chapter 5. It may reveal that the instruction being provided in science, for example, may fall short of GREAT instruction. In that case, the processes described earlier to change teacher practices should be focused in that subject. It might also reveal that a tier of interventions may need to be established in science for a small group of students.

How do you tell the difference between a deficiency in classroom instruction across the board and a need for a second tier of interventions? The answer lies in the percentage of students who are unsuccessful. If a large segment of the student population is unsuccessful, then the problem lies in classroom instruction. If a small percentage of students, perhaps 10–20 percent of the students exhibit difficulty, then the leadership team should focus on developing a tier of support for those students.

In some instances, schools confuse the two areas of need. When large numbers of students are having difficulty, they implement a layer of interventions in which students can be "double dosed" in that particular content area. For instance, students may receive a second segment of instruction in English rather than attending an elective class. The problem with this solution occurs when the problem is truly a core instructional issue and too few teachers are providing GREAT instruction.

The intervention, or the second segment of English in this case, looks very similar to the instruction provided during the student's first segment. The second dose suffers from less than GREAT instruction just like the first segment does. Therefore, the intervention is truly only allowing the student to have more time in the content area, not more specific instruction. The instruction provided by the teacher is not really enhanced.

If your school is implementing a "second dosing" approach to assist struggling students, then complete a data analysis to determine what percentage of the students taking that course are also required to take a second dose. If the percentage is quite high, take the steps outlined earlier to systematically change the practices of the teachers in the classrooms.

Once progress occurs on improving teacher practices, then establish a second tier of interventions that is more intensive and provides GREAT instruction at a higher level than that provided during the first dose of instruction. In many cases, a school will need to focus on both components—improving classroom instruction for all students and building a standard intervention protocol, second tier of intervention, for students that need additional support.

INDIVIDUALIZED INTERVENTIONS

Even when students are provided GREAT instruction and then a layer of standard interventions, such as tutoring or a minicourse, some students (granted, a relatively small percentage of those who have traditionally struggled) will still exhibit some difficulty. It is then time for a team of professionals to come together to analyze the barriers present for the individual student and to determine appropriate interventions for the student.

Many states have a standing team of educators who meet regularly to discuss students who experience difficulty. Depending on the state, this team may be referred to as the Student Support Team, the Teacher Support Team, or may go by another title. The main purpose of this group is not to be a stepping stone on the way for determining if a student has a disability or qualifies for another special program.

In fact, the purpose of this group is to dig a little deeper into individual student's performance to determine why the GREAT instruction and the standard layer of interventions have not resulted in sufficient progress. The purpose of this group, in fact, is to prevent a student from being unnecessarily labeled as having a disability or having another special label. The focus is on a review of the interventions and the development of instruction that will be uniquely tailored for each particular student.

Many times, students are discussed by the Teacher Support Team when they exhibit significant behavioral difficulties. Perhaps the student did not show acceptable behavior even when his classroom teachers clearly communicated behavioral expectations, taught those expectations to students systematically, and provided reinforcement and encouragement when those expectations were met. The student may have failed to demonstrate responsible behavior even when the instruction was engaging and differentiated through flexible groups. As a standard intervention, the student may have participated in a mentoring program provided by the school or a small counseling group provided by the school counselor. The student is still exhibiting behavioral challenges that cause his/her parents and the school staff serious concerns.

It may be time to conduct a Functional Behavioral Assessment. This terminology can be quite new, especially to educators who are not certified in special education, but it includes concepts that are often exhibited by outstanding teachers. In fact, you will see the results of a Functional Behavioral Assessment at your nearest church on Sunday morning.

The most difficult area to recruit volunteers in most churches is in the preschool program. Churches have to bend over backward to get volunteers to teach those classes. It can really be a challenge because the teacher sees the children only a couple hours each week and therefore has difficulty getting to know them, establishing expectations, or providing consistent reinforcement when those expectations are met.

In fact in almost every Sunday morning preschool, there is a three- or four-year-old student who is hardwired to be extremely active. Robert, for example, loves to move around the room and is continuously in motion. He bounces around the class, touches everything, and seems to have an inability to focus on any one task or sit still for longer than a minute. If the church is fortunate, there will be that fantastic teacher who conducts a Functional Behavioral Assessment without even realizing it.

Mrs. Lanier is one of those teachers. Before the Sunday school class starts, Mrs. Lanier walks with Robert to the field just outside of the preschool class. "Robert, I have this new watch and I haven't had a chance to use the stopwatch on it yet. I heard that you are an extremely fast runner. Can you run all the way around the field while I time you to see how fast you go?"

Of course, Robert is more than happy to show off his speed and takes a fast lap around the yard. "Robert, that was incredible. I didn't know you were that fast! I bet you can go even faster. Can you run around the field one more time and try to go even faster?" Robert is more than happy to oblige. After finishing his second lap, Robert is pretty tired and winded. "Robert, that was excellent. Can we go back into the classroom and would you like to have a seat so that we can read that story?"

Without even knowing it, Mrs. Lanier conducts a Functional Behavioral Assessment to determine the function of Robert's high activity. She determines that Robert is hardwired to crave physical activity. He is not happy or content unless he is extremely physically active. After determining the function of the behavior, it is easy for Mrs. Lanier to develop an appropriate intervention.

She decides to give Robert an opportunity to use all of his energy and need for physical movement in a constructive activity. By providing an opportunity to meet that need, Robert can then settle down and successfully participate in the Sunday school activities.

When the team of educators comes together to develop individualized interventions for a student with significant behavioral challenges, it is appropriate to discuss what happens before and after negative behaviors occur in order to analyze the function of the behavior (hence the name Functional Behavioral Assessment).

In all, there are two main purposes for misbehaviors: to either get something or to avoid something. The student may be attempting to avoid academic tasks that he/she feels are too challenging. The student may be attempting to avoid embarrassment from his classmates. The student may be avoiding attention from adults or peers.

Some students may exhibit troubling behavior because he/she may be seeking something like peer or adult attention. There are some students who continually seek attention and approval from their classmates. In middle schools, it is not uncommon for students to misbehave to earn credibility or acceptance from their peers. Jonah, for example, may be consistently argumentative with his teachers. If the teacher says something positive, Jonah dismisses it with something negative. He continually makes comments that interrupt instruction to earn a laugh from his peers.

It would be easy to fall into the pattern of punishing Jonah for repeatedly showing a lack of respect toward the adults in the room. The more skillful educators would conduct a Functional Behavioral Assessment and determine that Jonah is merely trying to gain positive attention from his peers. He is looking for reinforcement and acceptance from the girls and boys in the class.

Once the function of the behavior is determined, what would be an effective intervention? Ideally, the intervention would enable the student to obtain what he is seeking in acceptable ways rather than through misbehavior. It is clear that Jonah is going to get attention from his peers. The educators can either give him an appropriate avenue to get that attention or he is clearly going to do whatever it takes to earn that attention. If educators don't give it to him, then the student will take it.

The effective teacher will make it a point to talk to Jonah in private when the opportunity arises. In fact, it would be ideal if a new teacher could speak to Jonah before the first day of class. Mr. Pines may ask to speak to Jonah when he is seen in the hallway. "Jonah, I heard that you are going to be in my science class and I have heard about you." (Of course, Jonah will assume that his negative reputation has preceded him.)

"I have heard that you are a real leader. Other students seem to look up to you and want to be like you. I'm glad you are going to be in my class. I need a leader like you. Would you mind doing me a favor? I heard that you would be an outstanding leader for a discussion we will be having in our class about our recent weather patterns. If you spend a few extra minutes with me so we can discuss how to lead this group, would you like to lead this discussion in the class?"

By conducting a Functional Behavioral Assessment and developing interventions that meet the student's function of the behavior, Mr. Pines will give Jonah an opportunity to get what he is seeking, positive attention from his peers. He can gain that attention by showing responsible behavior rather than misbehavior. Jonah gets his need for attention met and the class has an opportunity to complete meaningful academic activities. Changing Jonah's behavior will not occur overnight. There are no magic solutions. But steadily providing replacement behaviors to gain the attention he seeks will improve his behavior.

The Functional Behavioral Assessments described here are fairly straight forward. An FBA can range from very informal and simple to a very standardized and complex process. The student's behavior and the difficulty or ease at which the functions of the behavior can be identified will determine the complexity of the Functional Behavioral Assessment.

This type of individualized intervention should be completed for students who exhibit academic deficits as well as those who demonstrate behavioral weaknesses. The team of educators should attempt to analyze the specific elements that create barriers for the student academically in order to determine interventions that target the student's particular needs.

Accountability for the Team

If your school includes a Student Support Team, Teacher Support Team, or a similar team that goes by another title, ensure that there are accountability measures built in. Ask the members of your Teacher Support Team for the data that summarizes the impact they have on the students in their caseload. Unfortunately, many teams will not be able to provide that data, or they will provide data that does not really answer the question.

Most Teacher Support Teams collect data on the number of students who are referred to their team and the number of students who are ultimately referred for additional testing to consider a specialized program like special education. Unfortunately, this data does not tell you about the impact the team's interventions have on their students.

Let's assume that 40 percent of a school's student population has been referred to the Teacher Support Team. Of those students, only 25 percent have been referred for a special-education evaluation. That information does not tell you if the interventions offered by the Teacher Support Team are being effective.

Some professionals might incorrectly assume that the data reveals that most students are responding positively to the interventions, because a relatively low percentage of students are considered for specialized interventions. Unfortunately, this data reveals that the school is not providing GREAT instruction regularly across the school since 40 percent of the students are not successful. The data does not provide any information on the effectiveness of the Teacher Support Team.

The Teacher Support Team should have a systematic process for analyzing the needs of each student and matching interventions tailored to meet the student's need. There should be a menu of specific instructional strategies that are considered when a fourth grade student is having difficulty with problem solving in mathematics. The Teacher Support Team should choose from those strategies in a systematic process.

They are then responsible for supporting teachers to ensure that the strategies are implemented with fidelity. It is safe to assume that the teacher may not be knowledgeable about the strategies or he/she would have already implemented them. The Teacher Support Team should provide training, support, and brainstorming with the teacher to ensure that he/she is equipped to deliver the strategy effectively.

The team should also be responsible for working with school administrators to develop a system of strategy monitoring. The team must ensure that the strategy is implemented over time with enough intensity and explicit instruction to make a difference with the student. That way, a solid analysis of the impact of the strategy can be completed. The team can determine if the strategy is or is not having an impact because they know that the strategy was implemented with fidelity over time.

The Teacher Support Team is then responsible for collecting data on the impact of each of the strategies on each student on their caseload. Therefore, when the administrators in the school ask to see the data that reflects the impact of the work of the Teacher Support Team, they can produce data that indicates:

- The specific weaknesses of each student,
- The interventions that were recommended for each student,
- That the teacher was provided training and support on the interventions,
- That the intervention was implemented with fidelity over time, and
- The impact of the intervention on the student's area of weakness.

SUMMARY

In order to meet the needs of almost all students, GREAT instruction must be provided in every class. But it should also be anticipated that some students will continue to have difficulties academically and behaviorally. Therefore, an effective school should develop predetermined interventions that are triggered for students when they exhibit difficulty. School personnel should analyze multiple years of data to determine specific areas that need to be addressed for many students throughout the school. Then, they should develop standard interventions that will meet the needs of those students (in addition to the GREAT instruction that is provided in every class). The effectiveness of the standard intervention should be systematically evaluated to ensure that it is enabling students to catch up to their peers. The ongoing analysis of the data will inform the continued implementation of the standard interventions.

Some students will require an additional layer of interventions tailored to the unique needs of the individual students. A team of educators should meet to analyze the core areas of weaknesses that interfere with the individual student's success and should develop interventions that target that student's unique needs. This Teacher Support Team should develop systematic processes for analyzing student's weaknesses, matching interventions to those needs, supporting teachers as they implement those strategies, monitor the implementation, and evaluate the impact of the strategies on the student's performance.

QUESTIONS FOR REFLECTION

Chapter 6: Build Tiers of Support for Struggling Students

1. In your school, in what specific areas have children tradition-ally shown weaknesses? Over the last few years, what percent of students have shown weaknesses in that area? If the per-centage is higher than 20 percent, describe the actions your leadership team will implement to move toward GREAT in-struction.

2. Does your school utilize a "double dosing" standard interven-tion approach for students who struggle? Does this interven-tion enable students who struggle to meet curricular expecta-tions? If you are unsure of the answer, how can you evaluate the effectiveness of your intervention?

3. How are the standard interventions in your school different from the typical classroom instruction? Are the interventions more intense and targeted than the typical classroom instruc-tion provided? If they are not, how can you adjust the inter-ventions so that they provide more intensive and targeted in-struction?

4. Describe the formative assessments that will be used for your standard tier of interventions. How will the schedule of the as-sessments and the response to the results of the assessments be more intensive than the formative assessments provided for all students?

5. In your school, do you have a process in which educators meet to brainstorm the individual needs of students who are consis-tently unsuccessful? In all honesty, does the purpose of that group seem to center on getting a specialized label on the stu-dent or analyzing the student's unique needs and developing interventions that will help the student in being successful?

6. Discuss the process that the group of educators uses to system-atically analyze the root causes of difficulty for students with behavioral difficulties and for those with academic difficulties. Are the two processes systematic (e.g., a Functional Behavioral Assessment) and do those processes lead to interventions that are individually tailored for each student? If not, how can those processes be more successful and systematic?

7. Ask the members of the Teacher Support Team for data that re-flects the impact they have on the students on their caseload.

Does the data provide sufficient information on student impact or is there a lack of appropriate data?

8. Has your Teacher Support Team collaborated with your administrators to develop a process by which teachers are trained and supported in the recommended strategies? Is there a process for monitoring the implementation of the strategies to ensure they are conducted with fidelity and sufficient intensity to warrant change in student performance? If not, describe how you will build those systems of support and monitoring.

9. Does your Teacher Support Team collect reliable data on the impact of the strategies on student outcomes? If not, develop a system in which data can be collected that will document that teachers have been trained and supported on the recommended strategies, the strategy implementation has been monitored, and the impact of the strategies on each student's performance.

7

Stop Doing Stuff
That Doesn't Help

The activities that are necessary to change adult practices so that GREAT instruction is implemented in every classroom have been discussed. Ultimately, the most important factor in radically increasing student achievement is to impact teacher practices. Some of the elements that we have covered will be time consuming, but they are all recommended because they will align all of the effort in the school toward improving student achievement.

One might wonder where all of the time will come from to implement these various activities with fidelity. Schools must stop engaging in activities that do not contribute toward improving instruction. In the example in the industrial sized kitchen in the second chapter, the novice cooks were working extremely hard, but they weren't being efficient in their task. It would be foolish and inaccurate for anyone to say that most school leaders and most teachers are not working hard. Unfortunately, much of that activity does not assist with fundamentally improving classroom instruction.

Time is our most important resource. It cannot be wasted by completing activities that will not contribute toward the ultimate goal of improved instruction. Therefore, the leadership team in your school must determine that activities described in this book will be implemented while activities that do not contribute toward the main vision will be completely discontinued if at all possible and mini-mized if they cannot be completely eliminated. A list of activities that should be eliminated or minimized in your school is provided.

DISCONTINUE INEFFECTIVE PROFESSIONAL DEVELOPMENT ACTIVITIES

Professional development systems that systematically improve the practices of teachers over time have been described earlier in this book. Effective professional development will include:

- Aligning all leaders in the school
- Aligning initiatives and programs throughout the school
- Establishing formative assessment for students
- Establishing regularly scheduled teacher meetings where teachers discuss their students' progress on formative assessments and how that information impacts the development of flexible groupings
- The implementation of research-based strategies with fidelity
- Explicit training on research-based strategies that allow teachers to delve deeply into the strategies over time to develop fidelity of implementation
- Nonjudgmental peer observations among teachers.

In order to change adult practices, it will take all of these components. Invariably, you will have people on your leadership team or in the school who will suggest that the school provide a one-shot training activity on a particular strategy or who will ask to attend a conference centered on a particular trend in education. These types of professional development activities do not improve teachers' or leaders' skills with fidelity any more than one lesson by the martial arts coach will improve Elisha's martial arts skills.

Financial and time investments in one-shot workshops, even if they cover multiple, consecutive days, rarely improve teacher practices. Let's pretend that a teacher or a leader actually asked the question with that information intact, "Can I attend a conference on a new instructional strategy that will take me out of the school for three days, that will cost a registration fee of a few hundred dollars, but will not change my practices with fidelity so it will ultimately have no impact on the academic achievement of my students?" Your answer as a school leader would most definitely be "no."

Unfortunately, professionals in education have been acculturated in an environment where a premium is placed on flashy one-shot workshops or conferences. Virtually every professional educational organization offers at least one conference a year. But if you ask the leaders of those organizations to show how those activities have impacted the practices of educators, they are unable to provide that data.

When most educators hear the term "professional development," they quickly envision a one-shot, "sit and get" workshop. Most educators will in fact tell you that professional development without ongoing coaching and support will not take root and change teacher practices, but requesting "training on" a particular strategy is the default for most educators. Since educators have usually been exposed to this type of one-shot training, they do not know how to develop a structure in which teachers and leaders will actually improve their skills through systematic approaches like the activities described throughout this book.

There are some instances when it is beneficial for specific faculty members to attend one-shot training activities. There are some professionals in schools whose position calls for an extremely specialized skill set that is not shared by anyone else in the building. Examples of these professionals include physical therapists, occupational therapists, teachers of students who are deaf/hard of hearing and communicate through sign language, and educational interpreters.

These individuals should certainly participate in the teacher groups and training activities that have been described in this book. They also need job specific training. They need training and support in those highly specialized skills in order to impact their practices and the achievement of their students. The tendency will be for them to participate in one-shot training activities or conferences put on by their respective professional organizations.

This approach has no more likelihood of improving their specialized practices than it does for classroom teachers who are larger in number. They need to develop ongoing relationships with experts in their respective fields and with their colleagues who have similar jobs in other schools or school districts. As a leader in your school, help these professionals in establishing supportive networks for themselves so they can continually brainstorm with their colleagues. Much of this type of brainstorming can be accomplished online with additional opportunities for these professionals to meet face to face perhaps in professional consortia.

When approached about attending a one-shot workshop that seems to provide specific information for these specialized professionals, ask them how they will access ongoing support, coaching, or brainstorming with like-minded colleagues as they implement the activities that are recommended at the conference.

MAKE ANNUAL PLANNING MEANINGFUL

Many schools have 3-ring binders filled with exhaustive School Improvement Plans. In many instances, these plans were developed by select individuals who worked in isolation and then combined their efforts for the submission to the school district's central office or the State Department of Education. Once they are developed, many of these plans sit on the shelf in administrators' offices and are only pulled down when they have to be updated.

Countless hours that went into developing School Improvement Plans are wasted because the final document does not truly drive reform in the school. In many cases, the School Improvement Plans are full of layers of data analysis with long descriptions of the activities and programs that are implemented in the school.

Many School Improvement Plans essentially include an expansive laundry list of the programs and initiatives within the school. Priorities are not evident. No program or activity seems more important than any other. With that type of planning, all activities in a school will be implemented in the same way they were the previous year— with the same results. The strategic planning process should clearly designate the priority areas for improvement based on student achievement. The areas of weakness should be precisely defined and a few specific and meaningful initiatives should be completed to address those weaknesses.

Any reader should be able to connect the specific areas of weaknesses with the logical and specific actions that will be implemented to address those weaknesses. The plan should include a description of how job-embedded professional development systems will be implemented so that teachers are more competent and effective at implementing the prioritized initiatives. Annual Plans are a case where less is truly more.

What happens when the school planning process lacks clarity and focus? The interventions are often not tightly aligned with the priority needs in the school. Take the example of Cooper Middle School. Cooper Middle School is a hypothetical middle school in a large, urban school district that has approximately 900 students in the 6th, 7th, and 8th grades. For the last several years, the school has failed to make Adequate Yearly Progress, landing it on the Needs Improvement list for 4 consecutive years.

The student body is evenly comprised of White, Hispanic, and African American students and virtually all of them are categorized as economically disadvantaged. Approximately 10% of the students are identified as having a disability. The State Department of Education reports the academic performance of several groups at Cooper: 1) All students, 2) Hispanic students, 3) African American students,

Table 7.1: Cooper Middle School: Three consecutive years—percentage of students who met/exceeded expectations in mathematics

Mathematics Percentage of Students who Met/Exceeded Expectations Year I					
All Students	Hispanic	White	African American	Students with Disabilities	Economically Disadvantaged
49.7%	49.7%	49.2%	50.0%	27.8%	49.2%

Mathematics Percentage of Students who Met/Exceeded Expectations Year II					
All Students	Hispanic	White	African American	Students with Disabilities	Economically Disadvantaged
44.9%	44.7%	44.2%	44.4%	25.6%	45.4%

Mathematics Percentage of Students who Met/Exceeded Expectations Year III					
All Students	Hispanic	White	African American	Students with Disabilities	Economically Disadvantaged
36.5%	36.2%	35.1%	35.2%	21.1%	37.0%

Table 7.2:   Cooper Middle School: Three consecutive years—percentage of students who met/exceeded expectations in language arts

Language Arts Percentage of Students who Met/Exceeded Expectations Year I					
All Students	*Hispanic*	*White*	*African American*	*Students with Disabilities*	*Economically Disadvantaged*
65.0%	64.9%	64.8%	65.2%	38.7%	63.7%

Language Arts Percentage of Students who Met/Exceeded Expectations Year II					
All Students	*Hispanic*	*White*	*African American*	*Students with Disabilities*	*Economically Disadvantaged*
64.9%	64.8%	65.0%	65.1%	39.2%	64.1%

Language Arts Percentage of Students who Met/Exceeded Expectations Year III					
All Students	*Hispanic*	*White*	*African American*	*Students with Disabilities*	*Economically Disadvantaged*
68.4%	68.1%	68.5%	70.0%	45.9%	67.9%

Table 7.3:   Cooper Middle School: Three consecutive years—percentage of students who were absent more than 15 days during the school year

Absentee Rates Percentage of students who were absent more than 15 days during the school year Year I					
All Students	Hispanic	White	African American	Students with Disabilities	Economically Disadvantaged
24.3%	23.9%	24.7%	23.6%	31.4%	25.3%
Absentee Rates Percentage of students who were absent more than 15 days during the school year Year II					
All Students	Hispanic	White	African American	Students with Disabilities	Economically Disadvantaged
21.7%	21.3%	22.2%	21.0%	32.8%	22.0%
Absentee Rates Percentage of students who were absent more than 15 days during the school year Year III					
All Students	Hispanic	White	African American	Students with Disabilities	Economically Disadvantaged
18.6%	18.5%	18.7%	17.0%	31.0%	18.5%

4) White students, 5) Students with disabilities, and 6) Students from economically disadvantaged circumstances. Three years of data are provided that indicate the percentage of students in each subgroup that met or exceeded expectations on statewide assessments in language arts and mathematics.

The State Department of Education also published the following data that reflects the percentage of students in each group that were absent for more than 15 days in the respective school year.

Additional data is also available. At Cooper Middle, 23 percent of students with disabilities spend at least 80 percent of their school day in general education classes. This is a reduction when compared to the two previous years.

When the leaders of Cooper Middle School were developing the School Improvement Plan, several initiatives were put into place. They decided to implement a gender-specific approach in their school. One third of the school was established as the girls' academic team while another third of the school was established as the boys' academic team. The remaining students participated in co-ed classes. It was also determined that all teachers would loop with the students. The 6th grade teachers would move to 7th grade when the students moved up at the end of the school year. They also implemented a double dosing opportunity for students in mathematics. Students who did not meet expectations on the statewide assessment in mathematics participated in an additional math class instead of participating in an elective course.

There are significant problems with Cooper Middle School's School Improvement Plan. The data are stunningly clear. In fact, it is very rare that quantitative data tell a story with such clarity. Cooper Middle School has major difficulties with achievement in mathematics. Since Year I, the percentage of students who have met or exceeded expectations on statewide assessments has dropped drastically. This pattern is evident across every subgroup.

This is in stark contrast to the performance of the students in language arts. For the two previous years, the data indicated relatively stable performance with an upswing for all subgroups during Year III. In fact, twice as many students met or exceeded standards in language arts than met or exceeded expectations in mathematics.

There are additional data pieces that may explain some of the underperformance at Cooper Middle School. Even though the absentee rate has improved over the last few years, a large percentage of students are excessively absent in all subgroups, especially students with disabilities. In addition, there is a very low percentage of students with disabilities who are being educated in general education classes when compared to the placement patterns for students with disabilities across the country.

When you consider the achievement data for Cooper Middle School, it is apparent that there is one area that clearly needs attention above all others—mathematics. However, the School Improvement Plan does not reflect this focus. The leadership team has decided to implement gender-based school teams. There may not be anything wrong with gender based education. In this case, it will only be effective at improving student achievement if it significantly improves the instruction.

At Cooper, an extremely high percentage of students do not meet expectations in mathematics across all subgroups. This typically indicates that teachers do not have sufficient knowledge in the content area, in this scenario—mathematics. Teachers do not have a deep and compelling understanding of the material that should be taught. They do not have expertise in the subject area and therefore are limited in delivering instruction that enables students to become sophisticated problem solvers.

With this lack of confidence in mathematics, teachers are providing surface level information with ineffective teaching practices. They are not providing instruction that is guided by a deep and thorough understanding of the curricular standards (the "G" in GREAT instruction). They are also not providing instruction using research-based instructional strategies that require students to participate in rigorous activities (the "R" in GREAT instruction).

It would not be a surprise to observe mathematics classes across the school and to find two strategies monopolizing classroom activities—teacher lecture and student independent work. If this is in fact the case, then students would certainly not be engaged or excited by their class work in mathematics (the "E" in GREAT instruction). One might also assume that neither the teachers nor the leadership team are using formative assessment data to guide instruction. They are not using ongoing assessment data to implement instruction in flexible groups tailored to meet the specific needs of their students (the "A" and "T" in GREAT instruction). Had they been doing so, the targeted instruction would have resulted in higher levels of achievement across the board.

The leaders at Cooper are attempting to improve mathematics performance by providing a second dose of instruction in mathematics. As mentioned in the previous chapter, it can be misguided to implement a 2nd tier of instruction that merely provides students more time with the same type of ineffective instruction that is already being provided. Select students at Cooper will need a 2nd tier of instruction, but the leadership team should focus extensively on the classroom instruction that is being provided throughout the school in mathematics.

With approximately 70 percent of the students failing to meet expectations, it is obvious that classroom instruction is falling far below the components of GREAT instruction. As they work to improve mathematics instruction across the school, they can build a 2nd tier of instruction that is even more intense and more targeted than the GREAT instruction provided across the school.

In addition to focusing on mathematics instruction, Cooper Middle School should implement activities to address two additional needs. They should continue to implement activities that reduce the high absentee rates. The school has made progress in this area for several subgroups. They need to intensify their efforts to hopefully make a more drastic reduction in absentee rates.

The leadership team also must analyze why the interventions that are showing some progress for other subgroups are not having a positive impact on the disability subgroup. They need to analyze why there is a lack of progress for these students. Perhaps there are students who have ongoing health issues that are interfering with their ability to attend school. In this case, the school leaders need to build support systems so that students can participate in instruction, perhaps through hospital/homebound services when they must be absent.

Perhaps there is a pattern of suspending students who exhibit inappropriate behavior. This cycle of ineffective interventions may be inflating absentee rates. By analyzing the core issues, the leadership team will be able to design and implement interventions that will encourage students to attend school regularly, thereby giving them access to GREAT instruction.

There is another weakness in Cooper Middle School's School Improvement Plan. They have plans to loop the teachers with each consecutive year. This approach is counterproductive when considering what it will take to steadily improve the practices of the teachers throughout the school. As mentioned in earlier chapters, teachers need the opportunity to learn about new practices, try out those practices, and analyze how those practices impact student performance. They need continuous opportunities to learn about the curriculum and to become more competent in that curriculum. They need the opportunity to brainstorm instruction with their peers and to learn formally and informally from those around them.

By utilizing a looping approach, the teachers will not be able to attain mastery of their content and pedagogy. Once they are gaining some traction and have made some real progress in their skillfulness and the ability to have a positive impact on student learning, they will have to start the process all over again as they learn new material for a different grade level. The looping approach will undermine the efforts to steadily and effectively improve the instructional practices of the teachers. Ultimately, Cooper Middle School is a clear example of a disconnection between the interventions and the school's needs. If the school implements its current plan, it will not make noticeable progress in student achievement.

There is another reason for developing School Improvement Plans that are concise and clear. All school stakeholders, including teachers, administrators, support personnel, central office staff, parents, and members of the community should be able to pick up the School Improvement Plan and clearly understand how the school has been performing and the priorities for the school over the next few years.

For all school personnel, the School Improvement Plan should represent their charge. It should be posted in every classroom and should drive the small and large group teacher meetings that were discussed earlier. It should clearly document the instructional strategies that will be undertaken during the year and the job-embedded professional development activities to be implemented in order to improve the practices of school personnel.

The Improvement Plan should function as a public relations document. It should explain the major goals for the school and in a digestible format explain how the school is planning on meeting those goals. An effective Action Plan is provided for Cooper Middle School.

Cooper Middle School Annual Plan of Action

Goals
Increase achievement in mathematics and language arts
At least 75% of the students in each subgroup of students will meet or exceed standards or there will be a reduction of 10% in the percentage of students in each subgroup that did not meet standards.

Reduce absentee rates
No more than 12% of students in each subgroup will be absent more than 15 days during the school year.

Increase the percentage of students with disabilities who are educated in general education classes
At least 45% of the students with disabilities will spend 5 of their 6 instructional segments in general education classes.

Current Status
- Over the last few years, the mathematics achievement of students in all subgroups has decreased consistently. In language arts, students' academic performance has remained relatively stable with an upswing last year. Approximately twice as many students demonstrate proficiency in language arts than math.
- Although there has been improvement for almost all subgroups, the student absentee rate continues to be excessive.
- The percentage of students with disabilities who are successfully educated in general education classes is below state and national trends.

Action Steps
- Mathematics teachers will consistently provide instruction, guided by performance standards, that requires the students to conduct sophisticated learning activities.
  - The mathematics coordinator for the school district will provide one hour of training every other week for all math teachers that will include practice in mathematics

content combined with investigations into research-based instructional strategies.

- The principal, mathematics department chair, assistant principal, and instructional coach will conduct two coaching observations a month with each mathematics teacher to assist them in incorporating their new skills.
- The results of common formative assessments will be reviewed every 3 weeks by teacher teams with a representative from the school's leadership team.
- Under the guidance of the department chair for language arts, the L.A. teachers will meet every other week to analyze the performance of their students and to discuss research-based instructional activities, guided by the curriculum, which will improve student performance.
- A positive, schoolwide initiative will be implemented that will provide rewards for each student who has not been absent during the month. Layers of interventions (mentoring, partnerships with parents, and more frequent rewards) will be triggered for students who miss more than 5 days of school prior to December.
- There will be four training activities for all teachers on differentiating instruction for students with disabilities. Ongoing coaching and support will be provided by the assistant principal and department chair for special education.

The Action Plan provides a clear and succinct road map that can be easily understood by all staff members and stakeholders. Instead of utilizing an Action Plan that describes all of the activities that will be conducted, Cooper Middle School clearly prioritizes those activities that will help them meet their school goals.

The Action Plan also reflects lots of work by the school staff. There are supporting documents that include a careful data analysis of student achievement and qualitative analysis of the school practices that are causing the student achievement levels, both good and bad. But the School Improvement Plan should be a document that propels action. Neither the school faculty nor members of the community are willing to wade through an expansive document to uncover the school's major goals or initiatives. This School Improvement Plan provides all stakeholders with their charge.

FOCUS ON INSTRUCTION, NOT PROCESS

In a previous chapter, I described how seemingly competing initiatives and programs are incongruent with systematically improving student achievement. Many of these initiatives are funded with different pots of money, such as the various Title programs, and therefore have different funding sources and different documentation requirements. The Title I program requirements, for example, are quite different from the special education program requirements.

This lack of alignment is complicated all the more due to the fact that the various programs are usually administered by different departments within a school district. Many of the district offices layer additional documentation requirements on top of the federal requirements, very often for very good reasons. The problem with all of these requirements is that it is extremely easy for school personnel to become focused on the process of administering the program rather than on the instruction that occurs on a daily basis in classrooms.

Special education is a prime example of this problem. Prior to the mid-1970s, school districts across the country were not obligated to provide services to students with disabilities. In 1975, the federal law entitled the Education for All Handicapped Children Act required that all school districts across the country educate all students with disabilities. With that law, which is extremely just, came layers of paperwork: student's evaluation process, individual planning activities for each student (called an Individual Education Program), and due process rights that ensure that students with disabilities are afforded a "free and appropriate public education."

Through the years, the federal legislation has been reauthorized, most recently in 2004, and is now referred to as the Individuals with Disabilities Education Act. In addition to the mandated processes that are established for every individual child, which becomes more complex with every reauthorization of the law, there are also requirements at the district level.

School districts must collect large data sets for reports such as the percentage of students with disabilities who are suspended or expelled for disciplinary reasons, the percentage of students with disabilities who are educated in general education classes for certain percentages of the day, and the ethnic distribution of various disabilities. Each program that receives funding from specific funding sources (federal, state, or local) requires certain processes and paperwork. These requirements serve a very specific purpose and can contribute extensively to the overall program's quality and accountability.

The data for students with disabilities can inform a school district that it is educating a higher percentage of students with disabilities in segregated, pull-out special education classes than other districts in their state and across the country. This is very meaningful information that can guide the school district in determining that equipping teachers to provide effective instructional programs for students with disabilities in general education classes is a priority.

Although the documentation and the required processes have a specific rationale and purpose, the sheer magnitude of the requirements can easily overshadow the instructional programs. Administrators, teachers, and parents can easily become bogged down in the administrative processes and lose focus on the real purpose of equitable education—to improve the achievement and opportunities for students with disabilities.

What should a school district or individual school do to remedy this problem? First of all, it is critical that specific members of the school district have a clear understanding of the origin and specific requirements of each program. Depending on the program in question, some of the requirements will be defined by the United States Department of Education with additional requirement perhaps added by the State Department of Education and the local school district. Some have been in effect for many years.

At the district level, personnel should have a deep understanding of the federal requirements. This should be the starting point. They should also consider how these requirements can be reported. Is the process at the district level for the schools more cumbersome than it has to be to meet requirements? Many times, especially as personnel changes occur at the school and district level, documentation and processes are maintained long after the original requirement has been removed. By having a deep understanding of the actual requirements from the funding source, school and district personnel can continually work to make the actual processes implemented in schools as streamlined as possible.

Ultimately, the implementation of processes should aim to meet the requirements as easily as possible while providing meaningful information that can continue to guide the school and districts' efforts. By minimizing the documentation and simplifying the processes, the district and school personnel can focus their time and effort on the instructional programs. Effort should also be placed into aligning all of the various documentation requirements.

FOCUS ON IMPROVING INSTRUCTION EVEN WHEN IMPLEMENTING STRUCTURAL CHANGES

Over the last decade many middle and high schools have transitioned from a schedule in which the students spent approximately one hour in each subject area to a block schedule in which students have extended time, perhaps 90 minutes to two hours in each academic period, with fewer classes each day. The rationale for the block schedule is there is time to delve deeper in the subject matter and complete more complex and rigorous activities. With the lengthened periods, teachers have the opportunity to provide hands-on activities in which students use critical thinking skills to apply the academic content.

In the schools where block scheduling changed instruction in that way, student achievement increased. In many schools, perhaps most schools that adopted block scheduling, classroom instruction did not change. Teachers provided the same instruction just for longer periods. Therefore, there was no significant increase in student achievement. Even though, there are some other benefits to block scheduling, such as a reduction in the amount of time that students spend in hallways, it is reasonable to ask whether the shift in the schedules and all of the person-hours that went into that effort were a good investment.

Initially, school leaders had to spend an extraordinary amount of time learning to organize their building in a block schedule. That activity, which seems natural at this point for many schools, involved a steep learning curve. School leaders had to reorganize how teachers and students were positioned on the school-wide schedule and how that schedule impacted all activities throughout the school. Teachers also participated in staff development activities regarding block scheduling. Entire faculties participated in workshops that described how this approach benefits students and faculties.

If there was not a corresponding change in student achievement (because instruction was not fundamentally changed), is it unreasonable to say that all of those person hours were wasted? There is nothing inherently wrong with either block scheduling or traditional scheduling, but this does illustrate the point that school improvement efforts that do not ultimately focus on improving classroom instruction will not have a noticeable impact on student achievement.

When implementing structural changes whether converting to block schedules, re-mapping the organization chart, or changing the graduation requirements, for example, maintain a diligent focus on improving classroom instruction. The school leadership team should not limit its evaluation of the structural changes to how well those changes are being implemented.

In the case of block scheduling, for example, do not merely evaluate whether teachers and students are adapting to their new schedule. Make sure that you evaluate the corresponding changes in classroom instruction and student achievement. Conduct classroom observations to ensure that teachers are implementing the various components of GREAT instruction with greater fidelity than they did when there was a traditional schedule. Also analyze formative and summative data to determine if students are exhibiting higher levels of achievement. Structural changes will not ultimately improve student achievement if there is not a consistent improvement in classroom instruction.

FOCUS ON CHANGING PRACTICES, NOT "CULTURE"

Many books have been written about our need to improve the culture of our schools. Administrators in schools that have traditionally shown systemic weaknesses discuss how they must change the culture of their school before they will see significant improvements in student achievement. This line of thinking dictates that culture must change before changes in instruction and student learning can be expected. The problem with this reasoning is that it is based on the premise that educators must somehow change the way they think before leaders can expect changes in their practices.

Another problem with this line of thinking is that a school's culture is very difficult to define. Some administrators will say that the culture of their school has improved when there is not a corresponding improvement in student achievement. *The truth is that a culture changes after adult practices are improved.*

A school's culture changes when teachers change from implementing weak instruction to implementing GREAT instruction and when the school's leaders spend their time building and implementing layers of support for that instruction. An improved culture is a side effect of drastically improving what happens in classrooms. By implementing systematic steps to improve instruction across the school, you ultimately impact culture.

QUESTIONS FOR REFLECTION

Chapter 7: Quit Doing Stuff That Doesn't Help

1. Consider the professional development activities that have been undertaken by your faculty. Have the professional development activities primarily focused on internal and external one-shot workshops? If so, were those activities effective at improving educators' practices and student performance? If not, describe why those professional development activities were ineffective.

2. Is your school's planning process effective or ineffective at focusing on specific instructional components that need improvement to enhance student achievement? Have you seen significant progress over the last few years or does the planning process seem ineffective at establishing a blueprint that will lead to observable improvements in instruction and thereby student performance? Explain your answer.

3. Is your School Improvement Plan a concise document that clearly describes the priorities for instructional improvement? Is that document used and understood by all stakeholders including administrators, teachers, students' families, and members of the community to drive their actions?

4. In your school, is there an imbalanced focus on processes rather than instruction? Does the completion of those processes seem

to have a positive or negative impact on student achievement? Describe how some processes can be eliminated or streamlined so that the school faculty can have an increased and diligent focus on instruction.

5. Describe some of the structural changes that have been implemented in your school during the last few years. Were those changes accompanied by corresponding improvements in classroom instruction? If not, describe why that is. Also describe how current structural changes can be used to further the cause of implementing GREAT instruction.

6. In your school, are you focusing on changing culture rather than changing adult practices? If so, describe how you can focus on changing adult practices (both teachers and leaders) toward GREAT instruction.

Conclusion:
Unrelenting Persistence

Throughout this book, it is clear that a school must diligently focus on providing GREAT instruction in order to radically improve student achievement. To be honest, it will take more than diligence. It will take persistence, unrelenting persistence. Countless initiatives, processes, and requirements will try to distract you. The daily demands of running a school will tempt you to lose your focus. Sometimes, well-meaning personnel with misaligned initiatives will try to take you off of your game.

You must show unrelenting persistence and not be deterred. You will not lose your focus. You will consistently lead your school toward GREAT instruction. As the leader of the team, you must create a consistent and coherent vision of the components of effective instruction for your leaders and your teachers. Then you must methodically build and implement systems of support so that all personnel gradually improve their practices.

You must not be satisfied with providing one-shot workshops and hoping that teachers implement better practices. You must build systems of ongoing professional development that include brainstorming, coaching, and support. You must monitor formative data to ensure that students master the curriculum. You must tirelessly focus on improving instruction in every classroom across your school. Your persistence must be wrapped up in a positive and contagious attitude. But, you must show uncompromising persistence nonetheless.

According to L. Brown (personal communication, January 15, 2004), every school improvement initiative needs a "project warrior" that will continuously carry the torch for the new effort. This person will not allow the school to lose its focus. He/she will maintain the momentum. They will ask their colleagues about implementation. They will review ongoing data. They will analyze both teacher practices and student performance. They will not let the initiative fade away to be replaced by the next initiative. They will stay the course.

All members of the leadership team, the principal, assistant principals, instructional coaches, and lead teachers, must be "project warriors" who show positive, unrelenting persistence in improving instruction. You must be the cheerleaders for every step of improvement activities. Each member of the leadership team must continually remind all personnel about what can happen in your school. When teachers and leaders are discouraged, you must remind them of the stakes and paint the landscape of possibilities. You must encourage them so that they believe that it can be done and provide gentle but real pressure to be sure it gets done.

Even when faced with setbacks that will inevitably come, you must continue to move the school forward with a diligent focus on improving instruction. You must be the coach, the cheerleader, and monitor. You must make it clear that you will not be distracted. You will not be sidetracked. You will develop GREAT instruction in every classroom. You will focus your school and you will radically improve student achievement.

You must also be the visionary. There are many schools that have a long history of poor performance. Those schools are often filled with personnel who cannot even envision the possibilities for their school. In some high schools, for example, administrators and teachers cannot see what a great high school can be. They assume that more than half of the students are just going to be disengaged. They assume that all classrooms must be filled with the teacher lecturing from the front of the room while a large percentage of the students disregard the instruction. Those teachers expect that students will not be enthralled with their work and they mark it as a successful day if there aren't any major disruptions in the class.

Your leadership must enlist the faculty in what is possible. High schools should be a place where students walk into their classrooms and jump into activities waiting for them. They should be working in large and small groups and discussing and solving complex problems in all subject areas. Students should be engaged in different sides of political arguments and get involved in different political causes. They should develop math skills and build complex structures to test out those skills. They should be engaged with great literature and compare the tone, message, and plot of historical literature with the work of contemporary authors. Students should be engaged with technology and use various technological applications to investigate, build, and share information in complex and exciting ways.

A high school student should have his/her school days filled with enlightening discussions, interesting investigations, and multifaceted demonstrations of what they have learned. Students should feel challenged and supported with novel and interesting activities as they pursue deep understandings of their content area. High schools can be exciting places where students enjoy their daily activities and grow academically and socially. In fact, all schools should fit this bill.

Your leadership team must clearly communicate the possibilities for all schools: elementary, middle, and high schools. You must give your faculty the permission to dream big, to envision what kind of school you can become. You must set a course and then be unrelenting in your persistence to create those practices in your school. You have to envision it, enlist others, and then make it happen. You have to provide great leadership so that you can have a school filled with GREAT instruction.

Appendix 1:
GREAT Instruction

GREAT instruction is:
Guided by the curriculum
Rigorous with research-based strategies
Engaging and exciting
Assessed continuously to guide instruction
Tailored through flexible groups

Appendix 2:
Effective Professional Development Systems

In order to steadily and systematically improve classroom instruction, school leaders must build effective professional development systems that include:

1. A clear and consistent vision of the expectations for GREAT instruction in every classroom.
2. A needs assessment, or data analysis, to determine the starting point for every school year.
3. A system of professional development activities that systematically moves teachers toward GREAT instruction.
4. Mechanisms to provide ongoing feedback and coaching to teachers utilizing all members of the school leadership team.
5. A system of progress monitoring to ensure that teachers gradually improve their classroom practices and that students' learning is on track to meet curricular expectations.
6. Structures so that teachers have the opportunity to formally and informally learn from each other as they work toward implementing GREAT instruction.
7. Personnel and financial resources that are aligned and focused on GREAT instruction, with minimal distractions and interference.

Appendix 3: Aligning the Leadership Team

The leadership team must be aligned to set the foundation for improving teacher practices. In preparation for improving classroom instruction, the leadership team must:

- Complete a data-based needs assessment to determine levels of student achievement and the effectiveness of classroom instruction in various subject areas.
- Develop a consensus on concrete, observable practices that should be seen in every classroom that demonstrates that instruction is:
  - Guided by the curriculum.
  - Rigorous with research-based instructional strategies.
  - Engaging and exciting.
  - Assessed continually to guide instruction.
  - Tailored through flexible groupings.
- Align all programs and initiatives in the school toward the goal of implementing GREAT instruction.

Appendix 4: Equipping Teachers to Implement GREAT Instruction

- Implement formative assessments.
- Utilize teacher teams to analyze the results of the formative assessments.
- With teacher teams, regularly brainstorm instructional strategies, including flexible grouping patterns, to respond to the results of the formative assessments.
- Provide professional development activities on specific research-based instructional strategies.
- Each member of the leadership team conducts observations and provides feedback to classroom teachers.

Appendix 5: Stop Doing Stuff That Doesn't Help

- Discontinue ineffective professional development activities.
- Make annual planning meaningful.
- Focus on instruction, not process.
- Focus on improving instruction even when implementing structural changes.
- Focus on changing practices, not "culture."

References

About the national reading panel. (2001). http://www.nationalreadingpanel .org/NRPAbout/about nrp.htm (accessed June 27, 2006).

Baron, K. June 20, 2007. Personal communication with the author.

Brown, L. June 15, 2004. Personal communication with the author.

Burrello, L., J. Burrello, and M. Friend. (1996). *The power of two: Making a difference through co-teaching*. Bloomington: Indiana University. Videotape.

Cranium (n.d.). Super Fort. http://store.cranium.com/catalog/product_ info.php?ePath=1_136&products_id=881 (accessed April 7, 2007).

Eggers, L. November 15, 1993. Personal communication with the author.

Engelmann S., P. Haddox, and E Bruner. *Teach your child to read in 100 easy lessons*. New York: Cornerstone Library, 1983.

Fuchs, L., and D. Fuchs. (n.d.). What is scientifically-based research on progress monitoring? http://www.studentprogress.org/library/articles .asp#formative (accessed May 6, 2007).

Georgia Department of Audits and Accounts. (2007). School improvement program. https://www.audits.state.ga.us/internet/pao/rptlist.html (accessed April 4, 2007).

Hart, B., and R. T. Risley. (1995). *Meaningful differences in the everyday experience of young American children*. Baltimore: Paul H. Brookes.

Holland, L. November 9, 2005. Personal communication with the author.

Marzano, R. J., D. J. Pickering, and J. E. Pollock. (2001). *Classroom instruction that works: Research-based strategies for increasing student achievement*. Alexandria, VA: Association for Supervision and Curriculum Development.

National Center on Student Progress Monitoring (n.d.). *Resources: Curriculum-based measurement at the secondary-school level.* http://www.student progress.org/library/articles.asp#formative (accessed May 6, 2007).

National Institute of Child Health and Human Development. (2000). *Report of the National Reading Panel. Teaching children to read: An evidence-based assessment of the scientific research literature on reading and its implications for reading instruction: Reports of the subgroups* (NIH Publication No. 00–4754). Washington, DC: U.S. Government Printing Office.

O'Connor, J. L., and L. C. Williams. (2006). *Students with disabilities can make AYP: What every school leader should know.* Atlanta: Georgia Department of Education.

O'Connor, J., B. Primm, and A. Nanda. (2008). *Catching falling stars: A practical model for using cross-age tutors to reduce reading failure in struggling primary grade students and proactively address ethnic disproportionality in special education referrals and placements.* Presented at the International Reading Association Annual Conference.

Showers, B. and B. Joyce. (1996). The evolution of peer coaching. *Educational Leadership* 53, 6 (March): 12–15. http://www.ascd.org/portal/site/ascd/ menuitem.459dee008f99653fb85516f762108a0c/ (accessed January 13, 2008).

South Carolina Department of Education. (n.d.) Curriculum specialists/Overview. http://ed.sc.gov/agency/offices/SQ/ci/cs/ (accessed April 4, 2007).

Thernstrom, A. and S. Thernstrom. (2003). *No excuses: Closing the racial gap in learning.* New York: Simon & Schuster.

U.S. Congress. Education for All Handicapped Children Act—P.L. 94–142. (1975).

U.S. Congress. Individuals with Disabilities Education Act—P.L. 108–446 (2004).

U.S. Congress. No Child Left Behind Act—P.L. 107–110 (2002).

U.S. Department of Education (2006). Highly qualified teachers for every child. http://www.ed.gov/nclb/methods/teachers/stateplanfacts (accessed May 4, 2007).

U.S. Department of Education, Office of Special Education and Rehabilitative Services, Office of Special Education Programs. (2005). *26th Annual (2004) Report to Congress on the Implementation of the Individuals with Disabilities Education Act,* vol. 1. Washington, D.C.

Villa, A., J. Thousand, and A. Nevin. (2004) *A guide to co-teaching: practical tips for student learning.* Thousand Oaks, CA: Corwin Press.

What Works Clearinghouse (n.d.) Who we are. http://www.whatworks .ed.gov (accessed June 22, 2008).

Woodcock, R. (1998). *Woodcock Reading Mastery Test.* Circle Pines, MN: American Guidance Service.

About the Author

John O'Connor has led school improvement initiatives at the state and local level during his 19 years in public education. He is currently the executive director for special services with the DeKalb County School System in metro Atlanta. In that position, he supervises the programs for approximately 15,000 students with disabilities and those who are English Language Learners. Prior to that position, he worked with the Georgia Department of Education for 9 years where he supervised school improvement initiatives that focused on improving student academic achievement, increasing students' responsible behavior, and incorporating effective instructional and leadership practices. He has provided training to over 100 school, district, state, and national audiences. In 2004, he was awarded the Outstanding Alumni Award from the College of School Psychology and Special Education, Georgia State University. John lives in Stockbridge, Georgia with his wife, Shawn, and two sons, J.T. and Luke. He can be reached at greatinstruction@bellsouth.net.